GREAT WORK JOURNAL

If found, please call:

STARTED: .... / .... / ....
ENDED: .... / .... / ....

Copyright © 2021 Amanda Crowell
All Rights Reserved
ISBN 13: 978-1-7373741-0-7 (trade hardcover)
Published by Amanda Crowell
amandacrowell.com
All trademarks and registered trademarks are the property
of their respective owners.
BOOK AND COVER DESIGN BY CB Messer
Printed in the United States of America

10 9 8 7 6 5 4 3 2 1

Dedicated to my clients, whose towering potential for
Great Work inspires my own.

You are destined to change the world for the better,
and I'm delighted to help.

Amanda

CONTENTS

Introduction 1
Quick Start Guide 3
Set your 90-day Goals 5
Reflect and Set Your Weekly Tasks 19
Reflect and Set Your Daily To-dos 35
Reflect on Your 90-day Goals 127
Notes 131

INTRODUCTION

"Align your time to your Great Work, and you will experience a life of joy, impact, and success."

The Great Work Journal™ is your magic elixir of success.

That's a bold statement, and I mean it! The Great Work Journal puts you back in control of your life by putting you back in control of your time. Whether you are building healthy habits, trying to save money, or learning to be more patient with your children, the Great Work Journal will help you do this Great Work without ever feeling overwhelmed.

It supports you to ask the big question: "What do I *really* want for my life? And *why* do I want it?" With that insight in hand, the Great Work Journal will then nag at you (in a good way!) until you are doing *real things* in your *real life* to build a life you love.

At the same time, the Great Work Journal supports you as you build your resilience, recover from burnout, and re-commit to a baseline of self-care from which your Great Work will flow.

At the deepest level, the Great Work Journal steers you toward your own, personal Great Work—work and hobbies that makes you feel alive, is grounded in your unique point of view, creates a body of work to share with the world, and pulls you into communities of awesome people doing amazing things. All while helping you shed the work that makes you feel a little bit dead inside. Pursuing your Great Work involves making a choice to be fully alive. The Great Work Journal will help make that possible.

When you align your time to your Great Work (and ditch the rest), it changes *everything*.

Let's get started.

QUICK START GUIDE

SET GOALS: Set aside an hour to determine your three goals.

WEEKLY TASKS: Once a week, set aside half an hour to reflect on last week and plan your upcoming week.

DAILY TO-DOs: Every day, find 10 minutes to plan your day and 10 minutes to reflect on your day. Some people do a 10 minute plan in the morning and a 10 minute reflection at night, while others prefer to do both in the morning. It's your choice!

REPEAT!

LIFE IS A REFLECTION OF WHAT WE ALLOW OURSELVES TO SEE.

—Trudy Symeonakis Vesotsky

SET YOUR 90-DAY GOALS

Every 90 days, you will set new goals. This is the fun part!

Here's how to get the most from these exercises:

⏱ Carve Out Time

Schedule an hour of quiet and uninterrupted time. You'll use it to plan your goals for the next 90 days.

🔨 Be Decisive

There are a lot of decisions to make in the first few exercises. Do NOT stress about your choices! Follow your intuition, be decisive, and know that whatever you choose will get you where you need to go.

☺ Be Realistic, but Not Right Away

Begin the vision work without ANY effort to be realistic. Plumb the depths of your desire and figure out what would delight you. What would get you out of bed? What would blow your mind?

👁 Know That a Great Vision Is One That Inspires You To Great Work

Your best visions will feel a little scary, and maybe a little cocky, selfish, or unrealistic. Don't shut yourself down! We'll find a way for you to pursue your Great Work without violating your values.

Want more guidance on how to begin? Grab the Great Work Resource Pack at amandacrowell.com/Great-Work-Journal

WEB OF LIFE

....

Let's start by identifying what matters most to you in your life and business.

Step 1: Read through the three lists below.
Step 2: Make this list your own: You can add any categories you feel are missing, break my categories apart, or smush two of my categories together. This is just a place to start.
Step 3: Choose 12 areas to include in your web of life on the next page.

♥ Relationships
- Intimate relationships
- Friendships
- Family
- Social life
-
-

$ Finances
- Budgeting
- Saving for _____
- Spending less $ on _____
- Long-term savings

♟ Self-Care
- Creativity
- Adventure
- Spirituality
- Hobbies
- Downtime
- Meditation
- Sleep
- Time Alone

♥ Health
- Healthy Diet
- Exercise
- Mental Health Support
- Medical visits
- Vitamins
- Vegetables

👓 Career
- New job
- Promotion
- Networking
- More challenge
- Less overworking
- Boundaries

Creating Your Web of Life

1. **Choose twelve areas of your life that matter to you from the lists on the preceding page.** Write one per circle in the Web of Life on page 10.
2. **Mark how satisfied you are in each area of your life** by placing a dot on the line between the word "low" and the circle. The closer to the word "low," the less satisfied you are. Connect the dots with a line to see your web of satisfaction.
3. **Rank order these from 1-12 according to their priority to you.** In the smaller outer circles, give each area a rank order. Force yourself to choose between items that feel identical in their priority to you.
4. **Notice what you notice.** Are there areas of your life that are high priority and low satisfaction? These might be areas where you could make some progress in the next 90 days.
5. **Choose five areas of your life where you would like to make some progress.** This can involve optimizing an area that is already strong, building up an area where you'd like to be stronger, or working on an area that is a high priority with lower than desired satisfaction. Write them on page 10, one per area in the "Good Life: One Year From Now."

The Web of Life can bring up a litany of "shoulds."

"I should be prioritizing this."
"I shouldn't care so much about that."
Don't listen to the shoulds!

Instead, listen to the voice of truth inside of you and believe what you hear.

YOUR WEB OF LIFE:

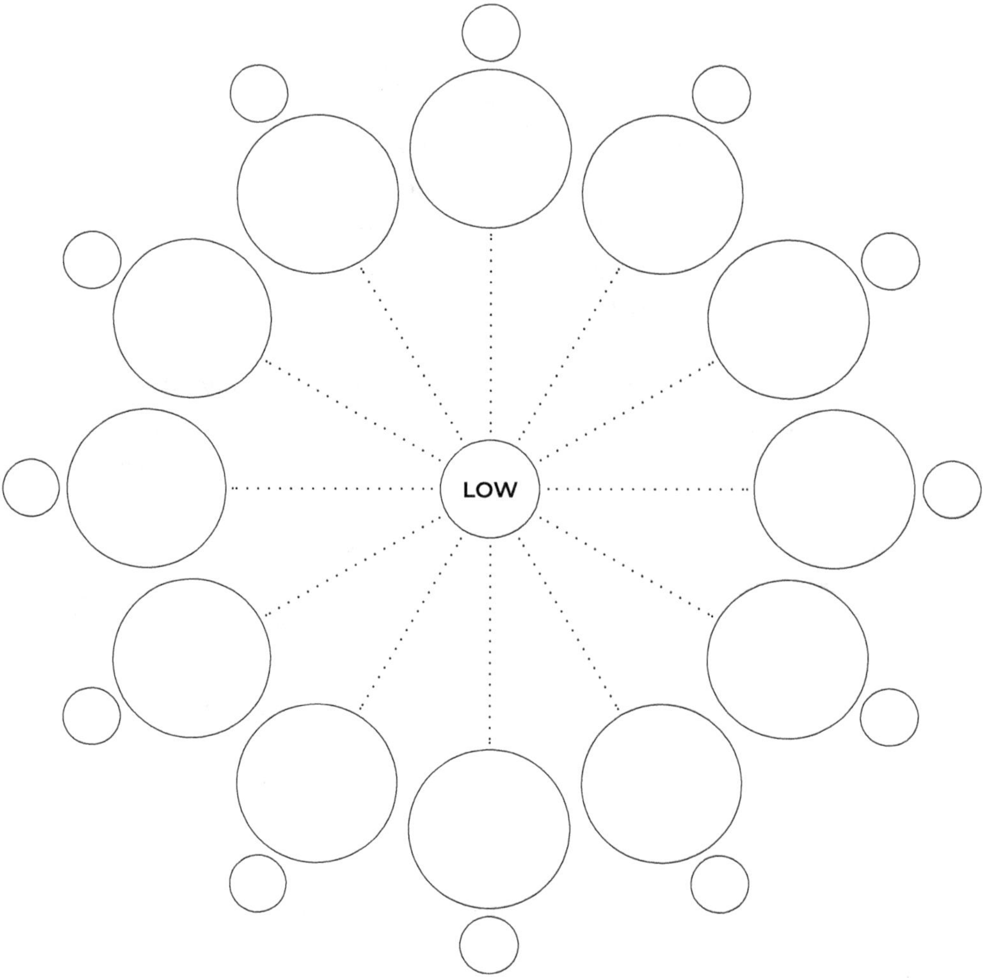

LOW

Choose five areas of your life in which you would like to make some progress. Write one per circle:

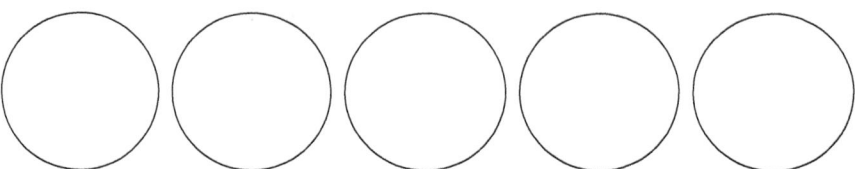

THE GOOD LIFE: ACCESSIBLE ASPIRATIONS

⚡ Brainstorm Instructions:

First, write the five areas you chose from your Web of Life in the five sections below.

Then, identify some one-year accessible aspirations for each:

📅 What do you want to be true in one year?
💗 What do you want your life to look like in one year?
🕊 What do you hope will happen in the next year?
🌱 To what do you aspire in the next year?

Think in term of concrete accomplishments and write them as if they are true.

For example: "One year from now..."

- I have nine clients
- I make $300,000
- I have finished the course I've been working on

⏱ **Take five minutes for each section and generate as many aspirations as you can.**

⭐ **Pro Tip:** Don't judge your brainstorm! Feel free to believe in the impossible and hope for the best. We'll be realistic when we're planning our goals, but when you are setting your vision, don't worry about "how" things will happen or "whether they're even possible." Also, don't worry if you "couldn't possibly do it all."

Right now, we are simply asking: **What do you want your life to look like in a year?**

GREAT WORK JOURNAL

Area 1: ....

Area 2: ....

Area 3: ....

Area 4: ....

Area 5: ....

Now, look over your brainstorm and **circle the three aspirations** that you are most excited to make progress on over the next 90 days. We will use these to create goals on the next page.

The Great Work Journal is built on the 3S Goal Structure: one goal that stretches you (Stretch), one that helps make the stretch possible (Support), and one that helps you feel grounded (Sanity).

An example:
I want to stop overworking and set some boundaries with my job. (Stretch) I will need someone to talk to about this, so I'll find a therapist and start meeting with her (Support). This is going to be hard, so I'm going to need something that makes it all worth it. I'm committing to going out with friends at least once a month (Sanity).

On the next page you will be asked to choose which of your three aspirations feels like a stretch goal, which feels like a support goal, and which one feels like a sanity goal.

★ **Pro Tip:** It helps to identify your chosen **stretch** goal first!

✋ **ON THE NEXT PAGE, WE ARE MOVING FROM BRAINSTORMING INTO CONCRETE GOALS WORK.**

NOW WOULD BE A GREAT TIME TO TAKE A BREAK.

THE NEXT 90 DAYS

FILL IN THE FOLLOWING BLANKS with the three aspirations that you are most excited to make progress on over the next 90 days.

★ **Pro Tip:** A smaller goal you can accomplish in 90 days is *always* better than a bigger goal that overwhelms you and could causes you to stumble.

◎ **Which goal?**   ○ Stretch   ○ Support   ○ Sanity
In one year, I aspire to:

How can I get a little closer to this in the next 90 days?

Is your goal concrete enough that you'll know when it's accomplished? If not, make it more measurable and specific.

Once you feel good about your goal, copy it onto the relevant goal planning page.

◎ **Which goal?**   ○ Stretch   ○ Support   ○ Sanity
In one year, I aspire to:

How can I get a little closer to this in the next 90 days?

Is your goal concrete enough that you'll know when it's accomplished?
If not, make it more measurable and specific.

Once you feel good about your goal, copy it onto the relevant goal planning page.

◎ **Which goal?**   ○ Stretch   ○ Support   ○ Sanity
In one year, I aspire to:

How can I get a little closer to this in the next 90 days?

Is your goal concrete enough that you'll know when it's accomplished?
If not, make it more measurable and specific.

Once you feel good about your goal, copy it onto the relevant goal planning page.

*You can have everything you want,
but not all at the same time.*

◎ **MY STRETCH GOAL FOR THE NEXT 90 DAYS IS:**

♥ Why does this goal matter to me?

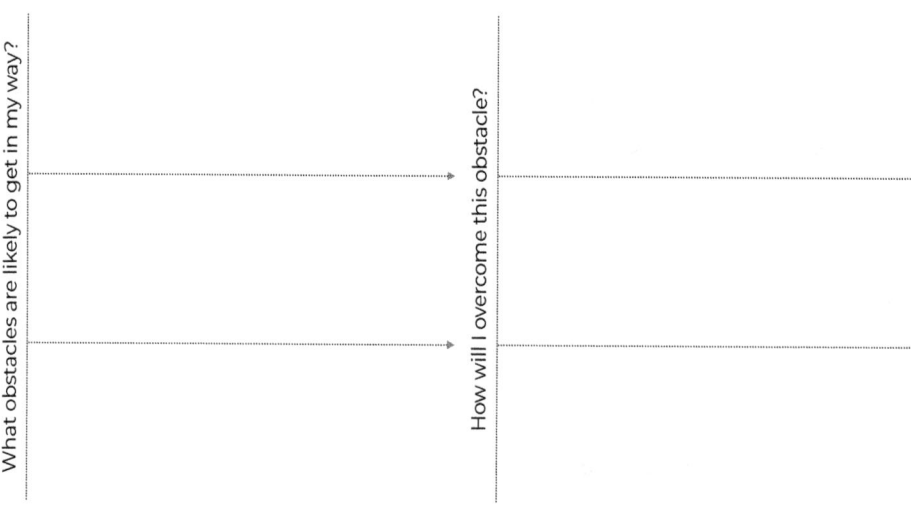

💧 What resources do I have to help me achieve this goal?
Who can I ask for help?

⚡ Brainstorm small steps that you can take right away. Whenever you get stuck, you can return to this list and begin again. Don't worry if you don't fill every line—as ideas occur to you over the next 90 days, you can add them to the list.

○ ....
○ ....
○ ....
○ ....
○ ....
○ ....

◎ MY SUPPORT GOAL FOR THE NEXT 90 DAYS IS:

♥ Why does this goal matter to me?

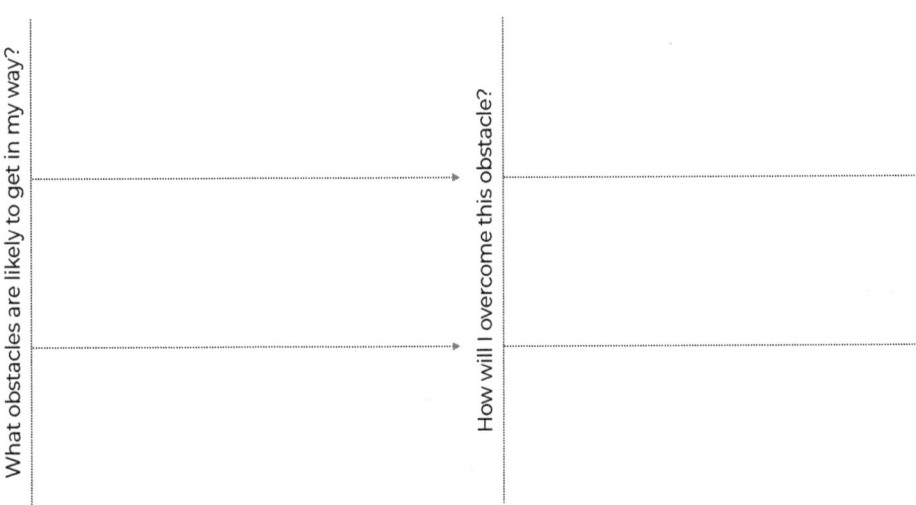

💧 What resources do I have to help me achieve this goal? Who can I ask for help?

⚡ Brainstorm small steps that you can take right away. Whenever you get stuck, you can return to this list and begin again. Don't worry if you don't fill every line—as ideas occur to you over the next 90 days, you can add them to the list.

○ ....
○ ....
○ ....
○ ....
○ ....
○ ....

◎ **MY SANITY GOAL FOR THE NEXT 90 DAYS IS:**

♥ Why does this goal matter to me?

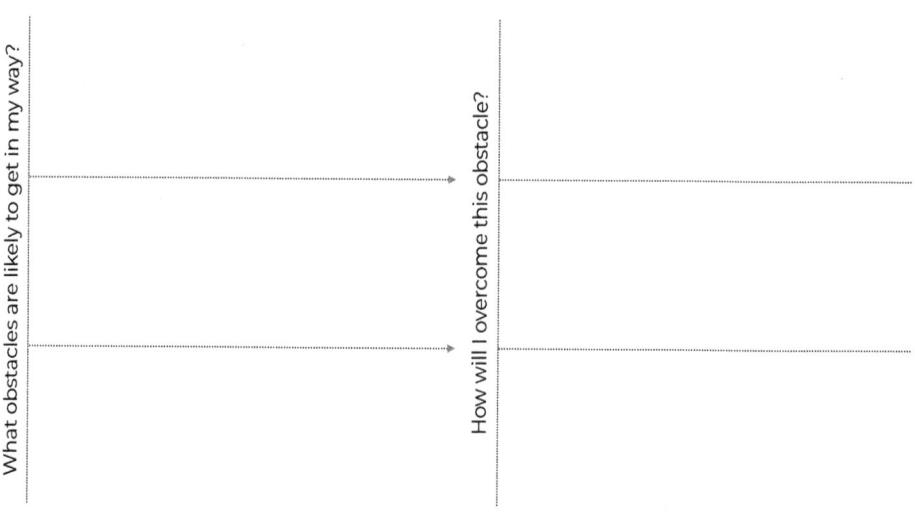

💧 What resources do I have to help me achieve this goal?
Who can I ask for help?

⚡ Brainstorm small steps that you can take right away. Whenever you get stuck, you can return to this list and begin again. Don't worry if you don't fill every line—as ideas occur to you over the next 90 days, you can add them to the list.

○ ....
○ ....
○ ....
○ ....
○ ....
○ ....

WANT MORE GUIDANCE ON HOW TO GET STARTED AND STAY MOTIVATED? GRAB THE GREAT WORK RESOURCE PACK

amandacrowell.com/Great-Work-Journal

NOTHING IS PARTICULARLY HARD IF YOU BREAK IT INTO SMALL JOBS.

—Henry Ford

REFLECT AND SET YOUR WEEKLY TASKS

Every week, you'll review the previous week and plan the next.

Here's how to get the most from your weekly practice:

↻ Make It a Habit

Schedule the time on your calendar to plan and reflect on your week. Give yourself about half an hour of quiet and uninterrupted time.

♀ Be Balanced

As you get started, it's useful to choose one weekly task for each of your three goals. This will help you quickly learn what it takes to make progress on these goals.

📅 Be Realistic

As you plan your week, make sure you consult your calendar and take on three tasks that can realistically be accomplished.

Note: If you find that you never have time to work on your goals, it might be time to set a weekly task to "say no, let go, or back out of some commitments."

⌛ Keep It Short

Reviewing the previous week and planning the next should take between 20 and 30 minutes.

✻ Bounce Back

If you forget to plan one week, don't worry! If you remember during the week, just plan for what's left. And if you forget even longer, don't try to go back! Just plan for whatever is left of your current week and keep moving forward.

○ I reviewed my 90-day goals

WEEK 1 .... TO ....
DATE RANGE

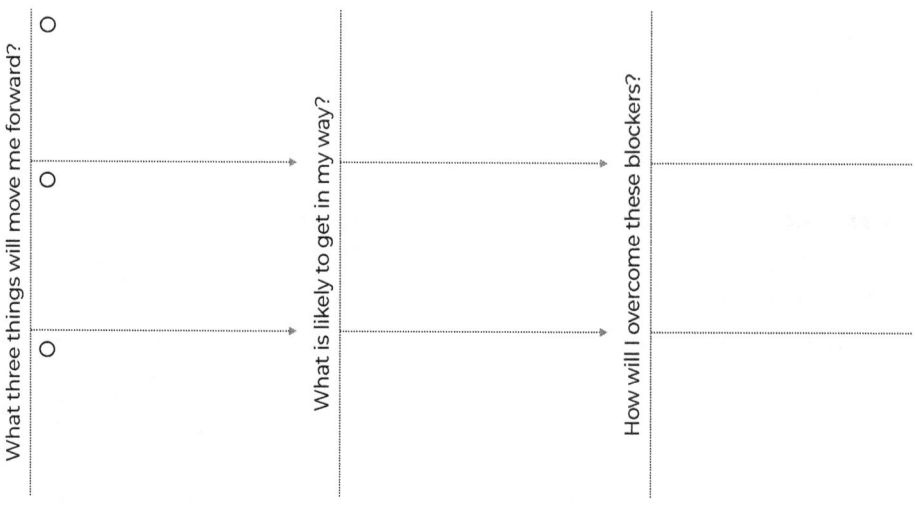

⊘ What will I say NO to this week?

🧍 How can I keep my life in balance this week?

📅 **WEEKLY REFLECTION**

🕘 What are my three favorite memories from this week?

1 | 2 | 3

✅ Did I do what I said I would do this week?
What can I learn from this?

🏃 How am I progressing against my 90-day goals?

○ I reviewed my 90-day goals

WEEK 2 _____ TO _____
DATE RANGE

⮕ **HOW CAN I GET A LITTLE CLOSER TO MY GOALS THIS WEEK?**

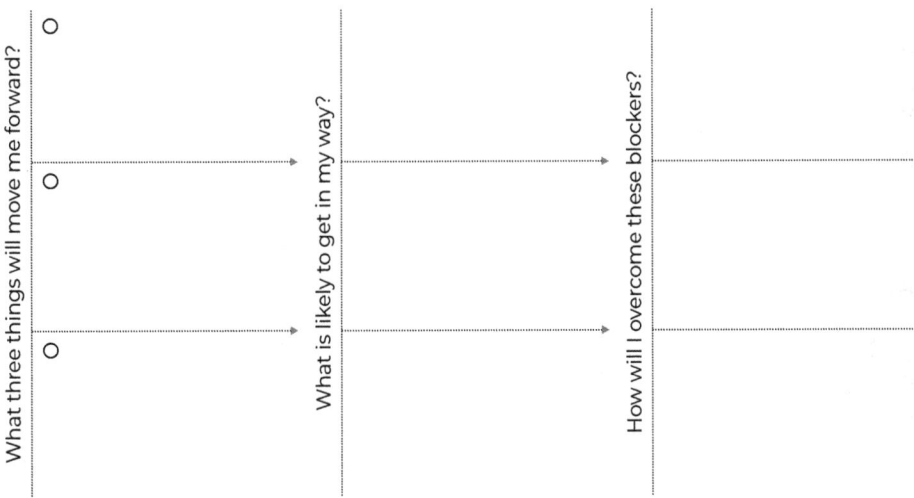

🚫 What will I say NO to this week?

🧍 How can I keep my life in balance this week?

📅 **WEEKLY REFLECTION**

🕘 What are my three favorite memories from this week?

1 | 2 | 3

✅ Did I do what I said I would do this week?
What can I learn from this?

🏃 How am I progressing against my 90-day goals?

○ I reviewed my 90-day goals

WEEK 3 .... TO ....
DATE RANGE

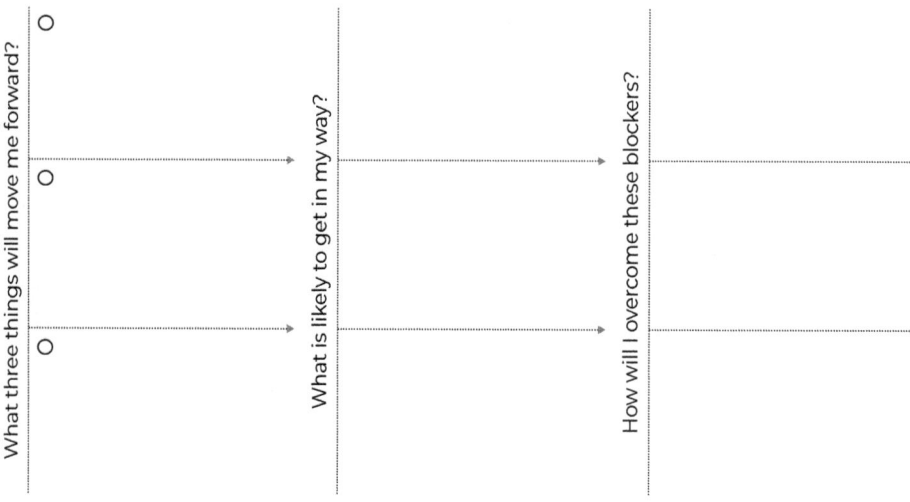

➤ HOW CAN I GET A LITTLE CLOSER TO MY GOALS THIS WEEK?

⊘ What will I say NO to this week?

🯄 How can I keep my life in balance this week?

📅 WEEKLY REFLECTION

🕚 What are my three favorite memories from this week?

1 | 2 | 3

✅ Did I do what I said I would do this week?
What can I learn from this?

🏃 How am I progressing against my 90-day goals?

○ I reviewed my 90-day goals

WEEK 4 .... TO ....
DATE RANGE

➡ **HOW CAN I GET A LITTLE CLOSER TO MY GOALS THIS WEEK?**

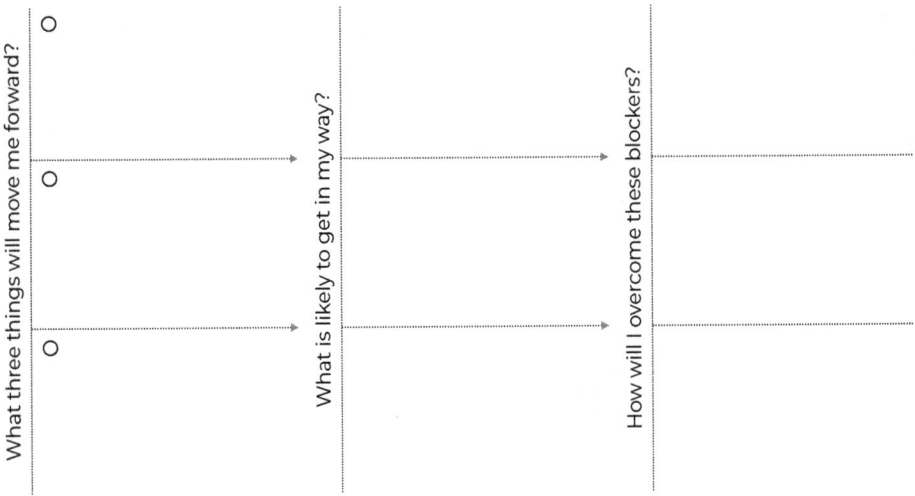

🚫 What will I say NO to this week?

🧍 How can I keep my life in balance this week?

📅 **WEEKLY REFLECTION**

🕐 What are my three favorite memories from this week?

1 | 2 | 3

✅ Did I do what I said I would do this week?
What can I learn from this?

🏃 How am I progressing against my 90-day goals?

○ I reviewed my 90-day goals

WEEK 5 .... TO ....
DATE RANGE

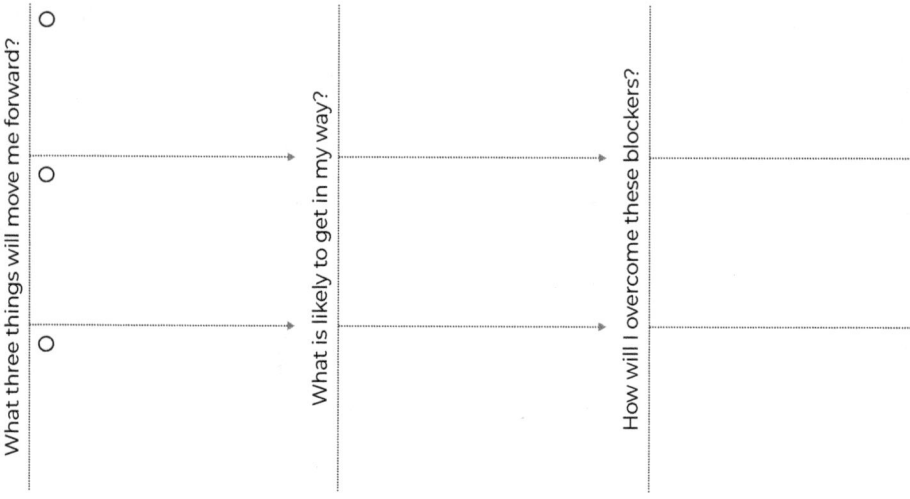

➡ **HOW CAN I GET A LITTLE CLOSER TO MY GOALS THIS WEEK?**

○ What will I say NO to this week?

🚶 How can I keep my life in balance this week?

📅 **WEEKLY REFLECTION**

🕒 What are my three favorite memories from this week?

1 | 2 | 3

✅ Did I do what I said I would do this week?
What can I learn from this?

🏃 How am I progressing against my 90-day goals?

○ I reviewed my 90-day goals

WEEK 6 .... TO ....
DATE RANGE

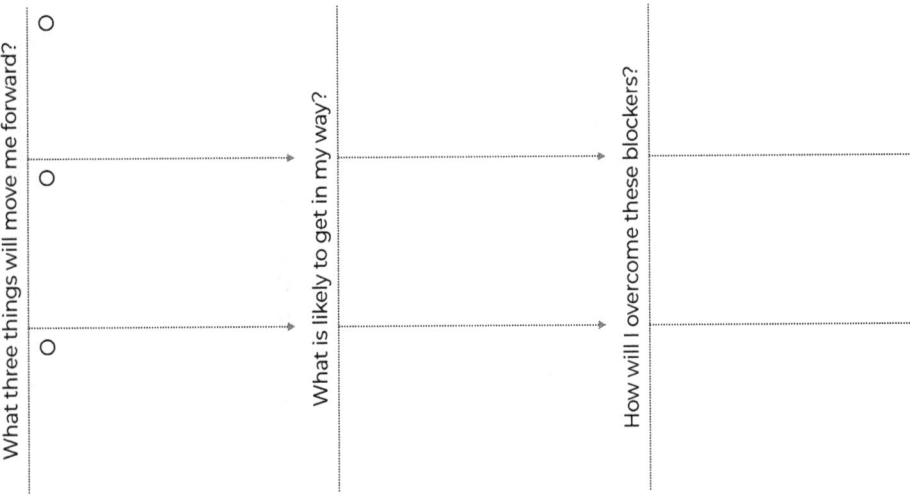

⊘ What will I say NO to this week?

🕴 How can I keep my life in balance this week?

📅 WEEKLY REFLECTION

🕗 What are my three favorite memories from this week?

1 | 2 | 3

✅ Did I do what I said I would do this week?
What can I learn from this?

🏃 How am I progressing against my 90-day goals?

○ I reviewed my 90-day goals

WEEK 7 .... TO ....
DATE RANGE

➲ **HOW CAN I GET A LITTLE CLOSER TO MY GOALS THIS WEEK?**

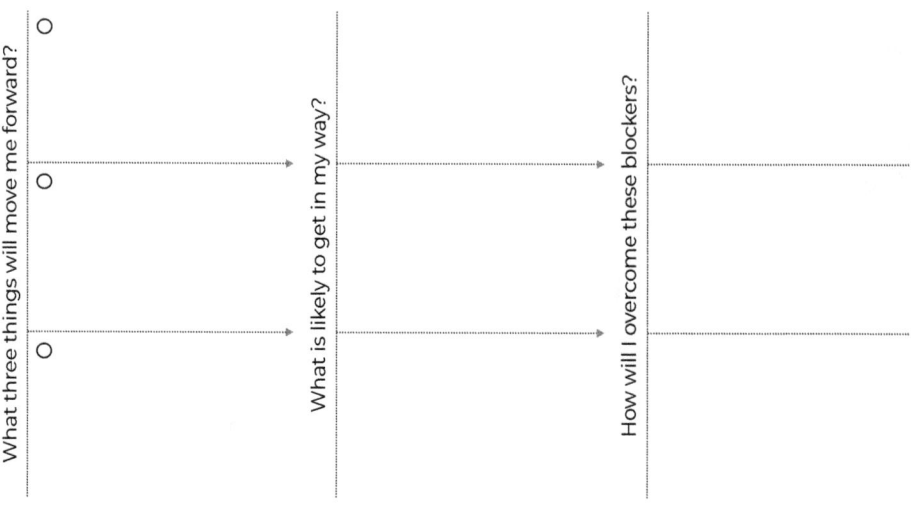

🚫 What will I say NO to this week?

🧍 How can I keep my life in balance this week?

📅 **WEEKLY REFLECTION**

🕗 What are my three favorite memories from this week?

1 | 2 | 3

✅ Did I do what I said I would do this week?
What can I learn from this?

🏃 How am I progressing against my 90-day goals?

○ I reviewed my 90-day goals

WEEK 8 _____ TO _____
DATE RANGE

➡ **HOW CAN I GET A LITTLE CLOSER TO MY GOALS THIS WEEK?**

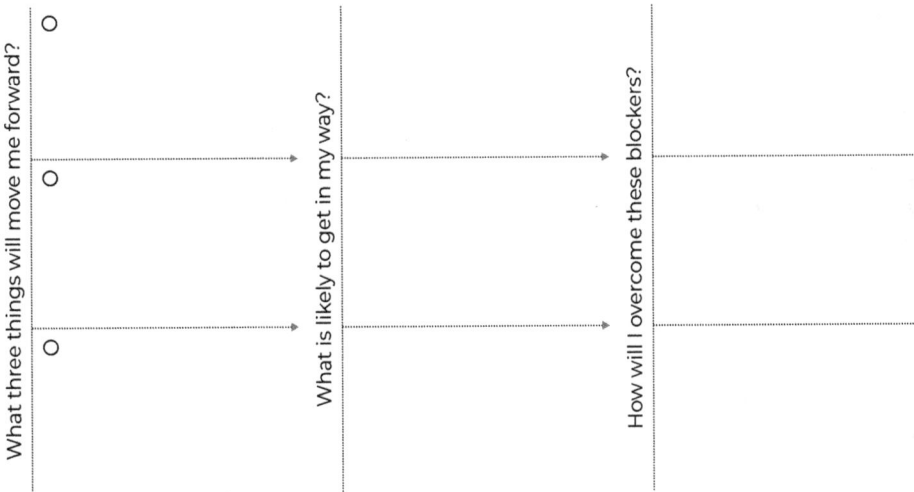

⊘ What will I say NO to this week?

👤 How can I keep my life in balance this week?

📅 **WEEKLY REFLECTION**

🕓 What are my three favorite memories from this week?

1 | 2 | 3

✅ Did I do what I said I would do this week?
What can I learn from this?

🏃 How am I progressing against my 90-day goals?

○ I reviewed my 90-day goals

WEEK 9 .... TO ....
DATE RANGE

➤ **HOW CAN I GET A LITTLE CLOSER TO MY GOALS THIS WEEK?**

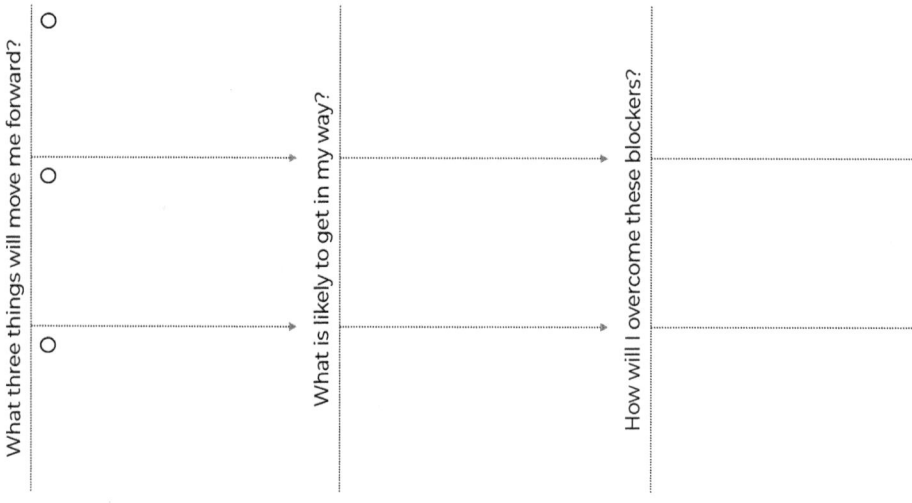

🚫 What will I say NO to this week?

🧍 How can I keep my life in balance this week?

📅 **WEEKLY REFLECTION**

🕘 What are my three favorite memories from this week?

1 | 2 | 3

✅ Did I do what I said I would do this week?
What can I learn from this?

🏃 How am I progressing against my 90-day goals?

○ I reviewed my 90-day goals **WEEK 10** _____ TO _____
DATE RANGE

➲ **HOW CAN I GET A LITTLE CLOSER TO MY GOALS THIS WEEK?**

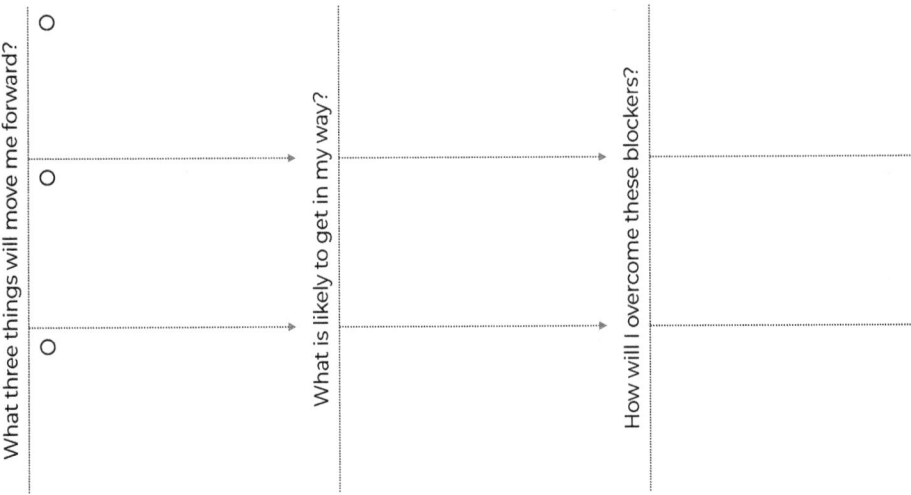

🚫 What will I say NO to this week?

🧍 How can I keep my life in balance this week?

📅 **WEEKLY REFLECTION**

🕘 What are my three favorite memories from this week?

| 1 | 2 | 3 |

✅ Did I do what I said I would do this week?
What can I learn from this?

🏃 How am I progressing against my 90-day goals?

○ I reviewed my 90-day goals

WEEK 11 .... TO ....
DATE RANGE

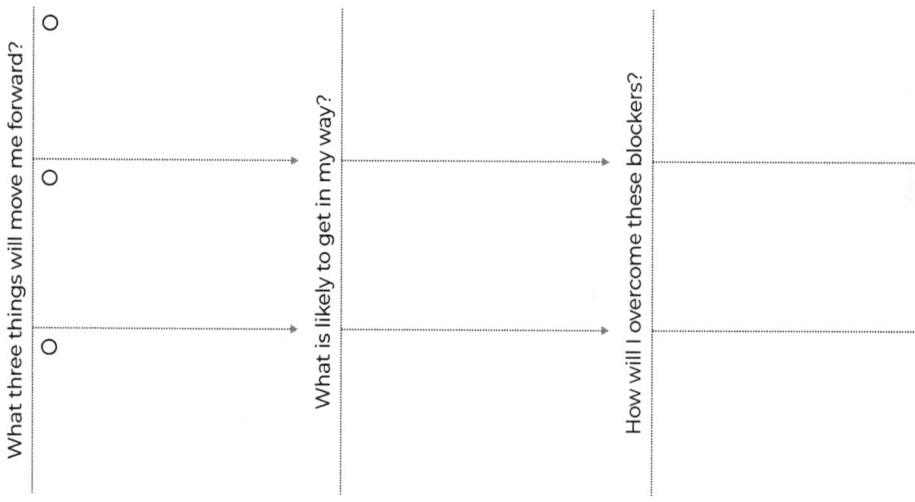

⊘ What will I say NO to this week?

👤 How can I keep my life in balance this week?

📅 **WEEKLY REFLECTION**

🕓 What are my three favorite memories from this week?

1 | 2 | 3

✅ Did I do what I said I would do this week?
What can I learn from this?

🏃 How am I progressing against my 90-day goals?

IT'S TIME TO REORDER!

amandacrowell.com/Great-Work-Journal

○ I reviewed my 90-day goals

WEEK 12 _____ TO _____
DATE RANGE

→ **HOW CAN I GET A LITTLE CLOSER TO MY GOALS THIS WEEK?**

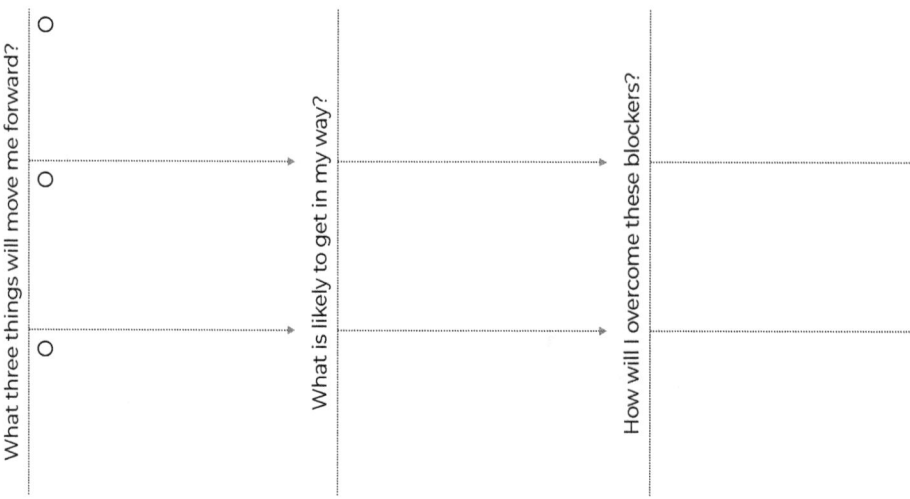

🚫 What will I say NO to this week?

🧍 How can I keep my life in balance this week?

📅 **WEEKLY REFLECTION**

🕒 What are my three favorite memories from this week?

1 | 2 | 3

✅ Did I do what I said I would do this week?
What can I learn from this?

🏃 How am I progressing against my 90-day goals?

○ I reviewed my 90-day goals

WEEK 13 _____ TO _____
DATE RANGE

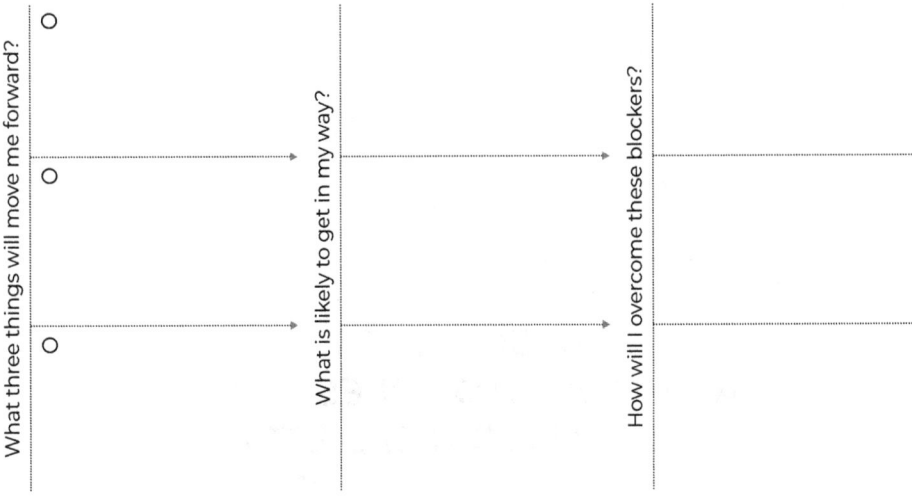

➔ HOW CAN I GET A LITTLE CLOSER TO MY GOALS THIS WEEK?

🚫 What will I say NO to this week?

🧍 How can I keep my life in balance this week?

📅 **WEEKLY REFLECTION**

🕓 What are my three favorite memories from this week?

1 | 2 | 3

✅ Did I do what I said I would do this week?
What can I learn from this?

🏃 How am I progressing against my 90-day goals?

**THE JOURNEY OF
A THOUSAND MILES BEGINS
WITH A SINGLE STEP.**

—Lao Tzu

REFLECT AND SET YOUR DAILY TO-DOS

This is where you align your time to your goals every day. It's the heart of The Great Work Journal experience.

Here's how to get the most from your daily practice.

⚓ **Create a *Convenient* Routine**

It's best to complete this activity at the same time and place each day. If such a time doesn't yet exist, try to create one with this practice. Daily reflection helps to anchor and calm you for your day.

📅 **Be Realistic**

As you plan your day, make sure you consult your calendar and take on three to-dos that can realistically be accomplished.

🏀 **Bounce Back**

If you fall out of the habit for a few days, don't worry! Don't try to catch up! Just start back up today and keep moving forward.

🪁 **Keep It short**

It should take about 10 minutes to plan your day, and 10 minutes to reflect upon your day.

⁞⁞ **When You Stumble, Go Smaller**

If you notice a pattern that something isn't getting done over multiple days, break it into smaller to-dos and give yourself a win.

○ I reviewed my weekly tasks

TODAY'S DATE ..../........./

♥ I am grateful for:
Because:

☀ HOW CAN I GET A LITTLE CLOSER TO MY GOALS TODAY?

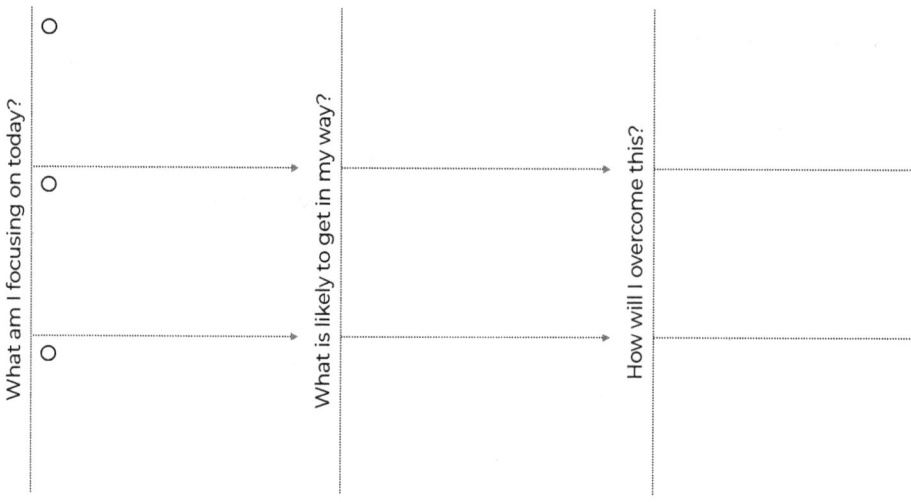

⊘ What will I say NO to today?

☾ DAILY REFLECTION

↺ What's my favorite memory from today?

✓ Did I do what I said I would do?
What can I learn from this?

○ I reviewed my weekly tasks   TODAY'S DATE ..../........../..........

♥ I am grateful for:
Because:

☀ **HOW CAN I GET A LITTLE CLOSER TO MY GOALS TODAY?**

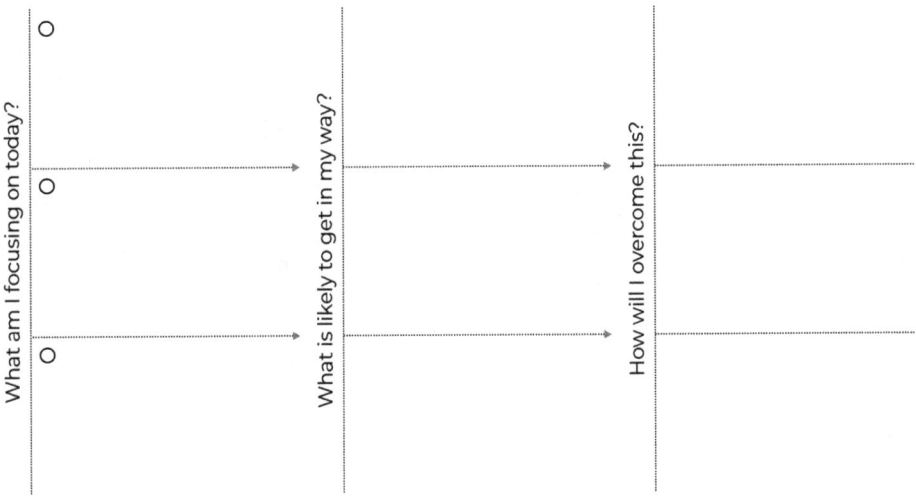

⊘ What will I say NO to today?

_____

☾ **DAILY REFLECTION**

🕗 What's my favorite memory from today?

✓ Did I do what I said I would do?
What can I learn from this?

○ I reviewed my weekly tasks   TODAY'S DATE _____/_____/_____

♥ I am grateful for:
Because:

☀ **HOW CAN I GET A LITTLE CLOSER TO MY GOALS TODAY?**

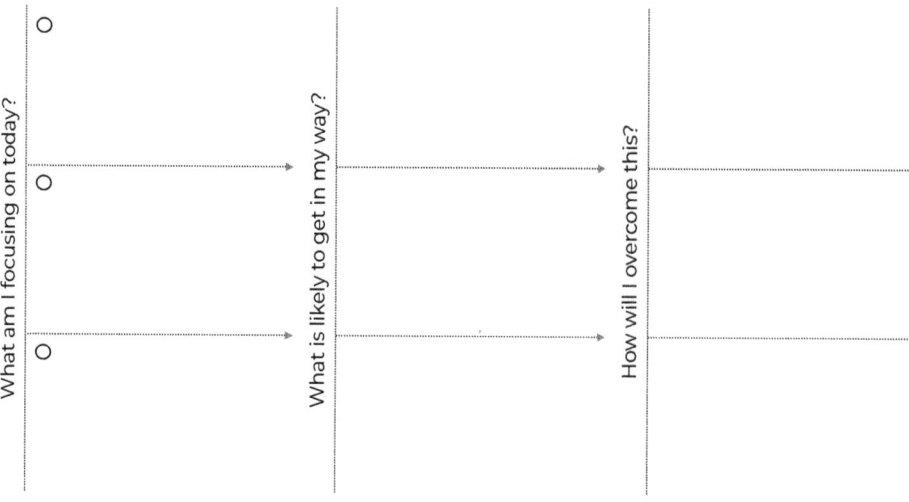

🚫 What will I say NO to today?

🌙 **DAILY REFLECTION**

🕘 What's my favorite memory from today?

✓ Did I do what I said I would do?
What can I learn from this?

○ I reviewed my weekly tasks   TODAY'S DATE _____ / _____ / _____

♥ I am grateful for:
Because:

☀ HOW CAN I GET A LITTLE CLOSER TO MY GOALS TODAY?

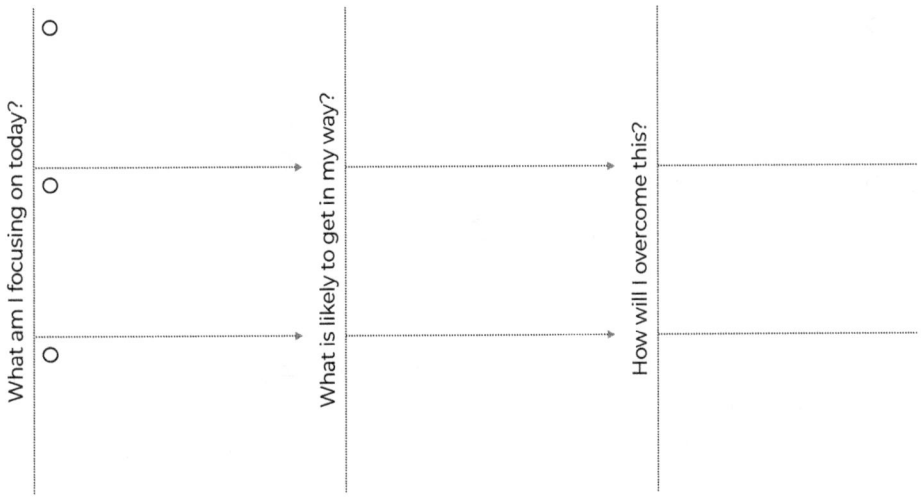

🚫 What will I say NO to today?

☾ DAILY REFLECTION

🕗 What's my favorite memory from today?

✅ Did I do what I said I would do?
What can I learn from this?

○ I reviewed my weekly tasks   TODAY'S DATE ..../........./.........

♥ I am grateful for:
Because:

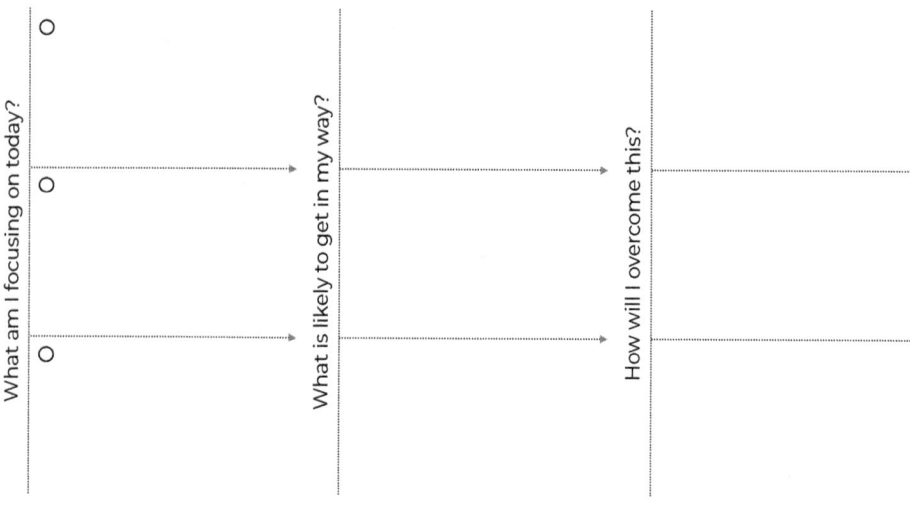

☀ HOW CAN I GET A LITTLE CLOSER TO MY GOALS TODAY?

○ What will I say NO to today?

☾ DAILY REFLECTION

⟲ What's my favorite memory from today?

✓ Did I do what I said I would do?
What can I learn from this?

○ I reviewed my weekly tasks   TODAY'S DATE _____ / _____ / _____

♥ I am grateful for:
Because:

☀ **HOW CAN I GET A LITTLE CLOSER TO MY GOALS TODAY?**

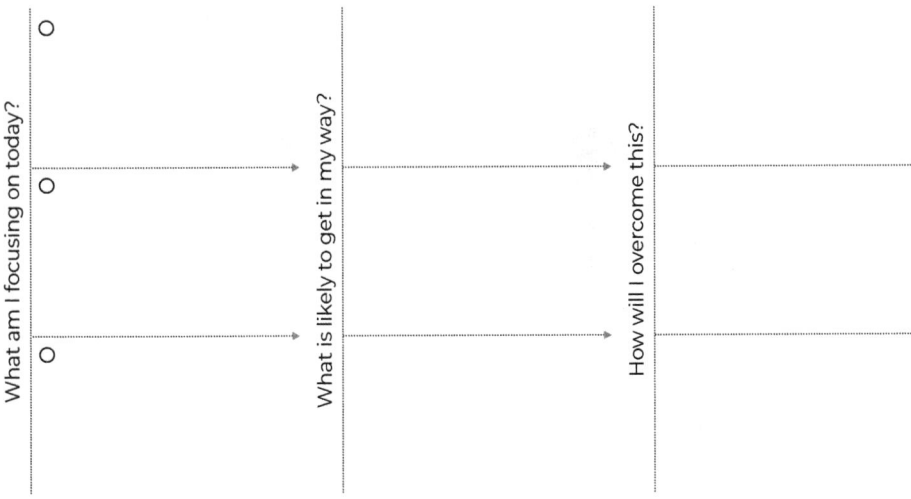

⊘ What will I say NO to today?

☾ **DAILY REFLECTION**

↺ What's my favorite memory from today?

✓ Did I do what I said I would do?
What can I learn from this?

○ I reviewed my weekly tasks   TODAY'S DATE ..../........../..........

♥ I am grateful for:
Because:

☀ **HOW CAN I GET A LITTLE CLOSER TO MY GOALS TODAY?**

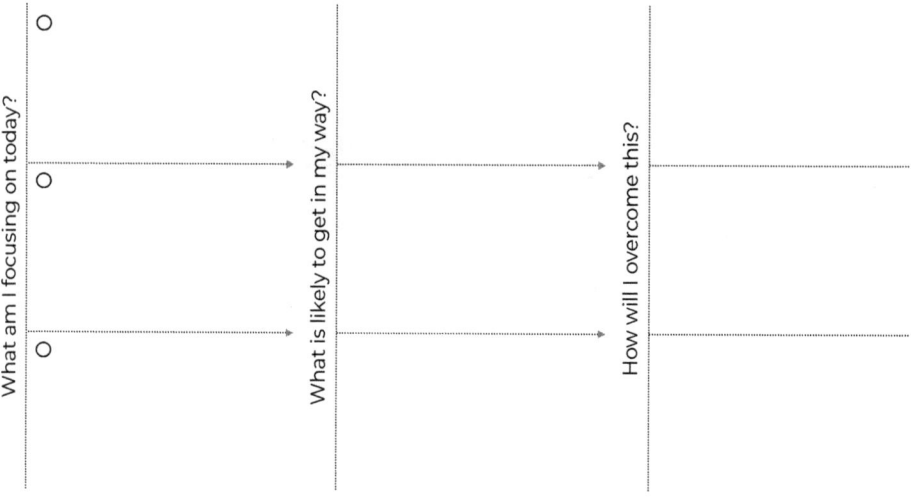

🚫 What will I say NO to today?

☾ **DAILY REFLECTION**

🕒 What's my favorite memory from today?

✓ Did I do what I said I would do?
What can I learn from this?

○ I reviewed my weekly tasks   TODAY'S DATE _____ /_____ /_____

♥ I am grateful for:
Because:

☼ **HOW CAN I GET A LITTLE CLOSER TO MY GOALS TODAY?**

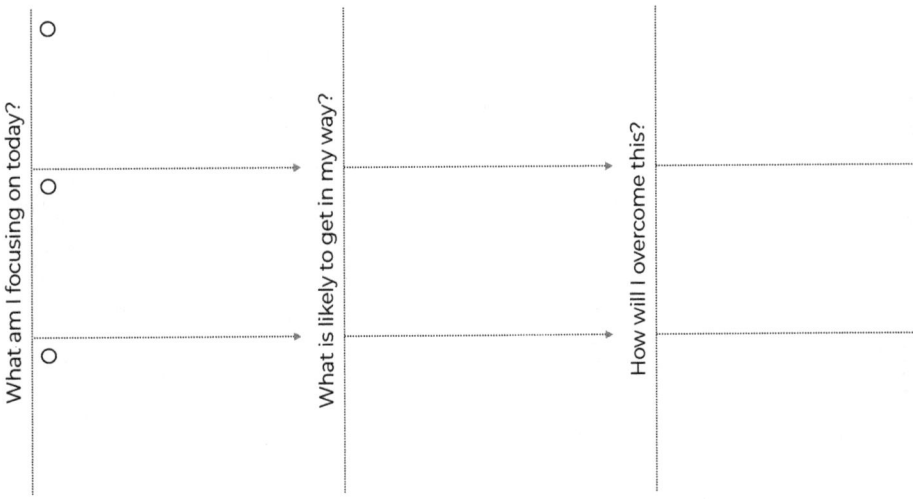

🚫 What will I say NO to today?

☾ **DAILY REFLECTION**

🕑 What's my favorite memory from today?

✅ Did I do what I said I would do?
What can I learn from this?

○ I reviewed my weekly tasks   TODAY'S DATE _____ / _____ / _____

♥ I am grateful for:
Because:

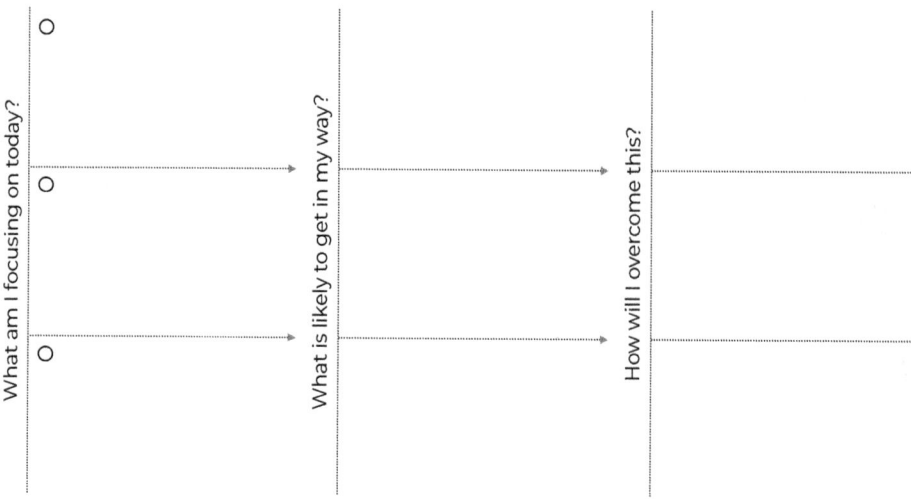

☼ HOW CAN I GET A LITTLE CLOSER TO MY GOALS TODAY?

⊘ What will I say NO to today?

☾ DAILY REFLECTION

🕒 What's my favorite memory from today?

✓ Did I do what I said I would do?
What can I learn from this?

○ I reviewed my weekly tasks   TODAY'S DATE _____/_____/_____

♥ I am grateful for:

Because:

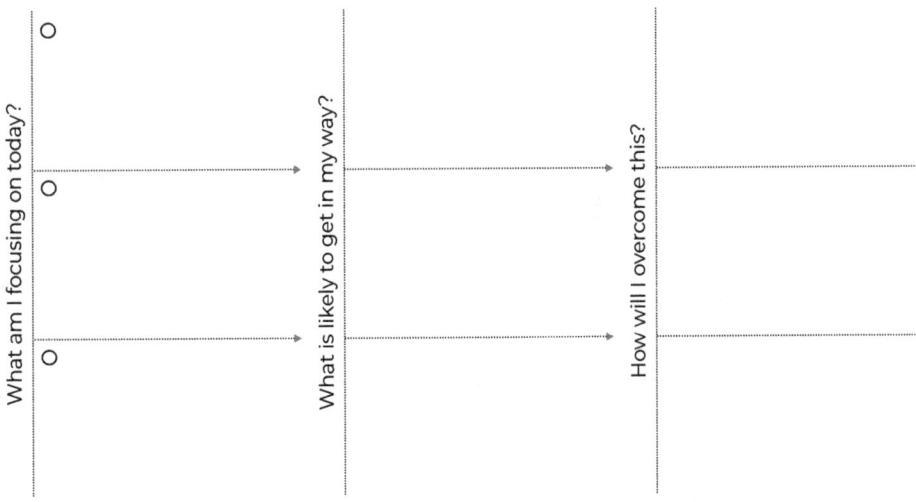

☼ HOW CAN I GET A LITTLE CLOSER TO MY GOALS TODAY?

What am I focusing on today?

What is likely to get in my way?

How will I overcome this?

⊘ What will I say NO to today?

☾ DAILY REFLECTION

⟲ What's my favorite memory from today?

✓ Did I do what I said I would do?
What can I learn from this?

◯ I reviewed my weekly tasks   TODAY'S DATE ..../........../..........

♥ I am grateful for:
Because:

☀ HOW CAN I GET A LITTLE CLOSER TO MY GOALS TODAY?

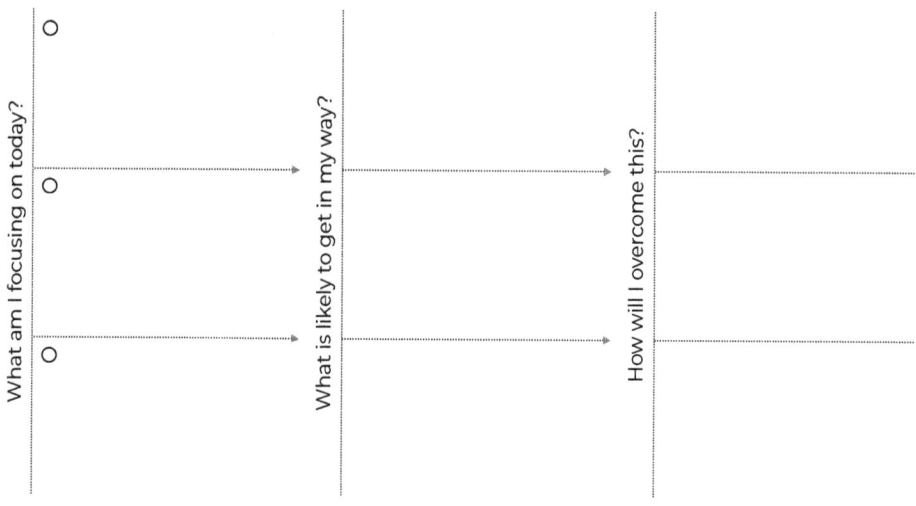

🚫 What will I say NO to today?

☾ DAILY REFLECTION

🕓 What's my favorite memory from today?

✅ Did I do what I said I would do?
What can I learn from this?

○ I reviewed my weekly tasks

TODAY'S DATE .... / .... / ....

♥ I am grateful for:

Because:

☀ **HOW CAN I GET A LITTLE CLOSER TO MY GOALS TODAY?**

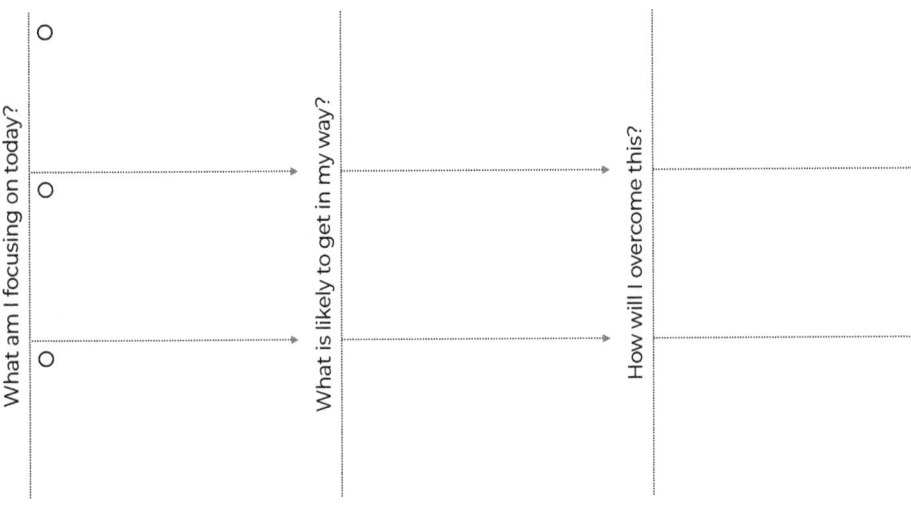

🚫 What will I say NO to today?

🌙 **DAILY REFLECTION**

🕘 What's my favorite memory from today?

✅ Did I do what I said I would do?
What can I learn from this?

○ I reviewed my weekly tasks   TODAY'S DATE .... / .... / ....

♥ I am grateful for:
Because:

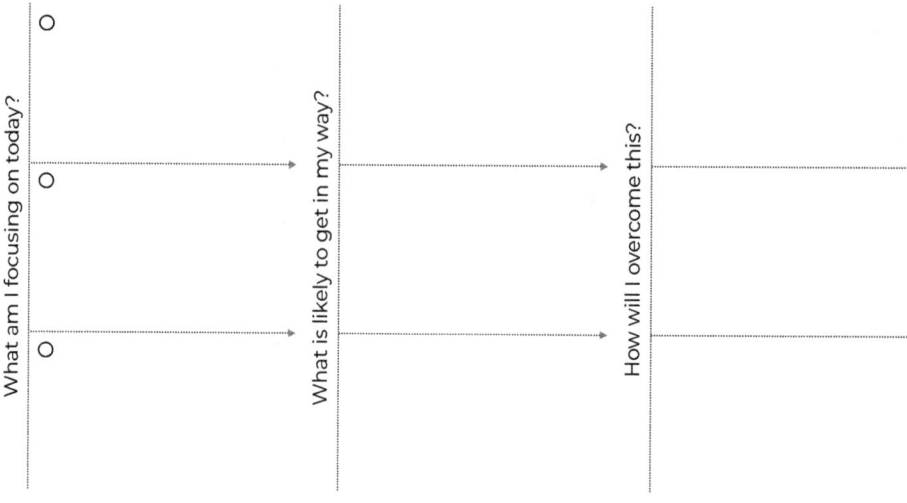

☼ HOW CAN I GET A LITTLE CLOSER TO MY GOALS TODAY?

🚫 What will I say NO to today?

☾ DAILY REFLECTION

🕒 What's my favorite memory from today?

✅ Did I do what I said I would do?
What can I learn from this?

○ I reviewed my weekly tasks   TODAY'S DATE ..../........./.........

♥ I am grateful for:
Because:

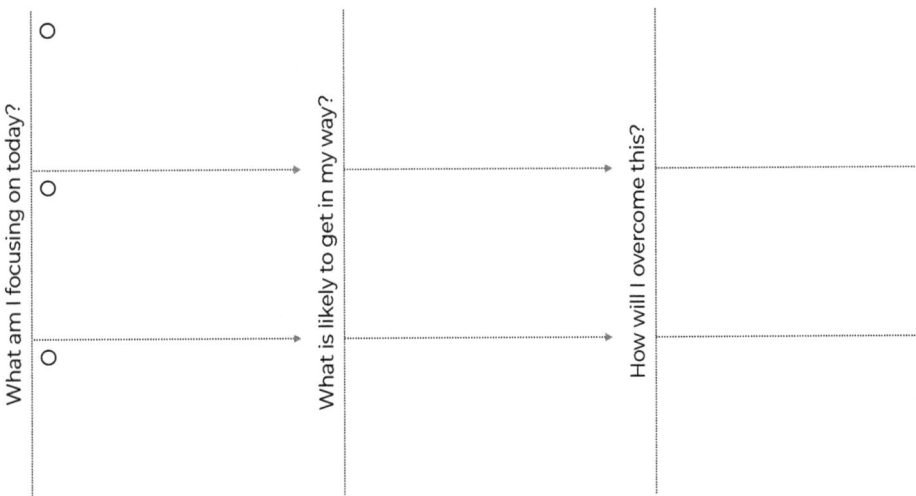

☀ **HOW CAN I GET A LITTLE CLOSER TO MY GOALS TODAY?**

🚫 What will I say NO to today?

☾ **DAILY REFLECTION**

🕗 What's my favorite memory from today?

✓ Did I do what I said I would do?
What can I learn from this?

○ I reviewed my weekly tasks   TODAY'S DATE ..../........../..........

♥ I am grateful for:
Because:

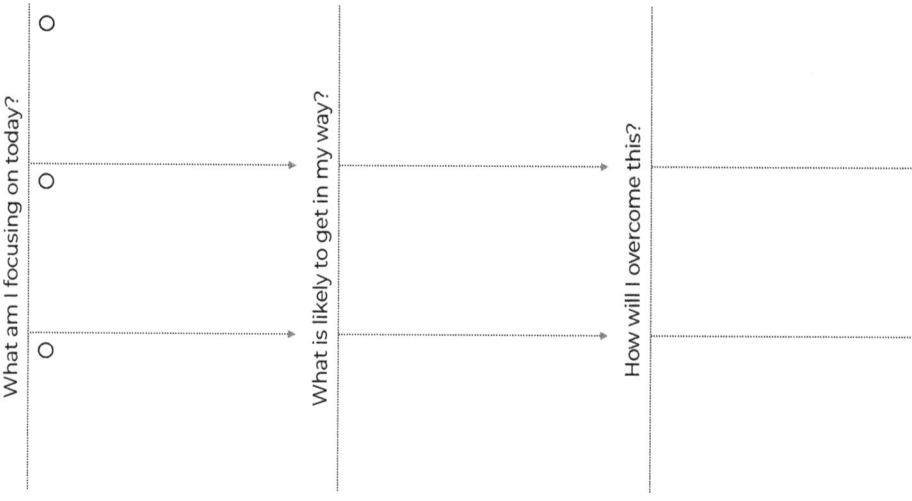

☀ HOW CAN I GET A LITTLE CLOSER TO MY GOALS TODAY?

⊘ What will I say NO to today?

☾ DAILY REFLECTION

🕓 What's my favorite memory from today?

✓ Did I do what I said I would do?
What can I learn from this?

○ I reviewed my weekly tasks

TODAY'S DATE ..../........../..........

♥ I am grateful for:
Because:

☀ **HOW CAN I GET A LITTLE CLOSER TO MY GOALS TODAY?**

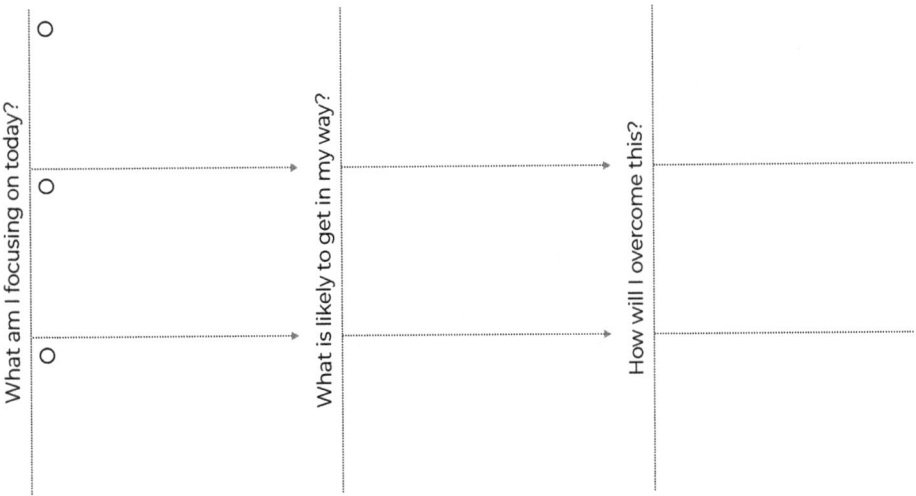

🚫 What will I say NO to today?

_____

☾ **DAILY REFLECTION**

🕘 What's my favorite memory from today?

✓ Did I do what I said I would do?
What can I learn from this?

○ I reviewed my weekly tasks   TODAY'S DATE ..../.........../...........

♥ I am grateful for:
Because:

☼ HOW CAN I GET A LITTLE CLOSER TO MY GOALS TODAY?

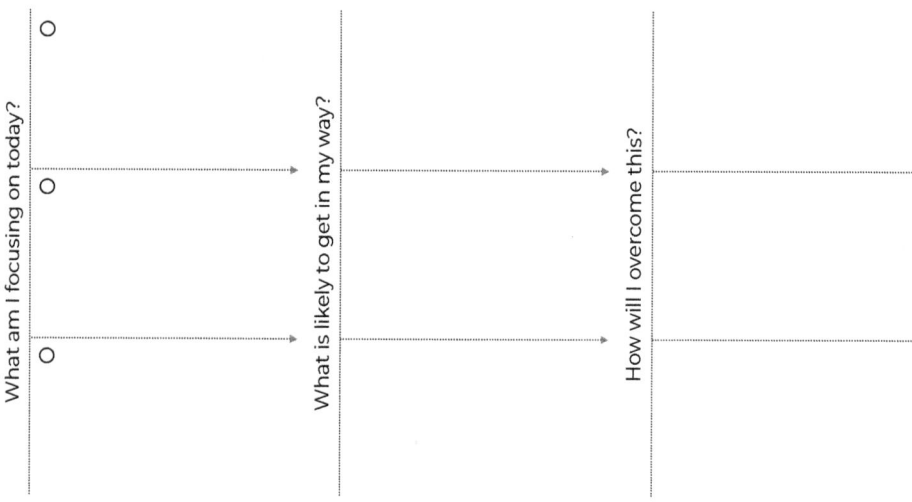

🚫 What will I say NO to today?

☾ DAILY REFLECTION

🕘 What's my favorite memory from today?

✅ Did I do what I said I would do?
What can I learn from this?

○ I reviewed my weekly tasks   TODAY'S DATE .... / .... / ....

♥ I am grateful for:
Because:

☀ **HOW CAN I GET A LITTLE CLOSER TO MY GOALS TODAY?**

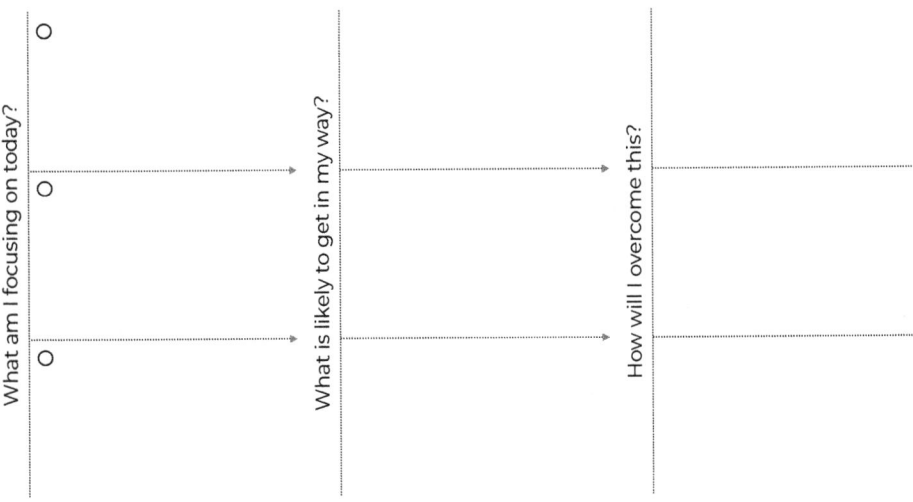

🚫 What will I say NO to today?

___

☾ **DAILY REFLECTION**

🕗 What's my favorite memory from today?

✅ Did I do what I said I would do?
What can I learn from this?

○ I reviewed my weekly tasks   TODAY'S DATE _____/_____/_____

♥ I am grateful for:
Because:

☀ HOW CAN I GET A LITTLE CLOSER TO MY GOALS TODAY?

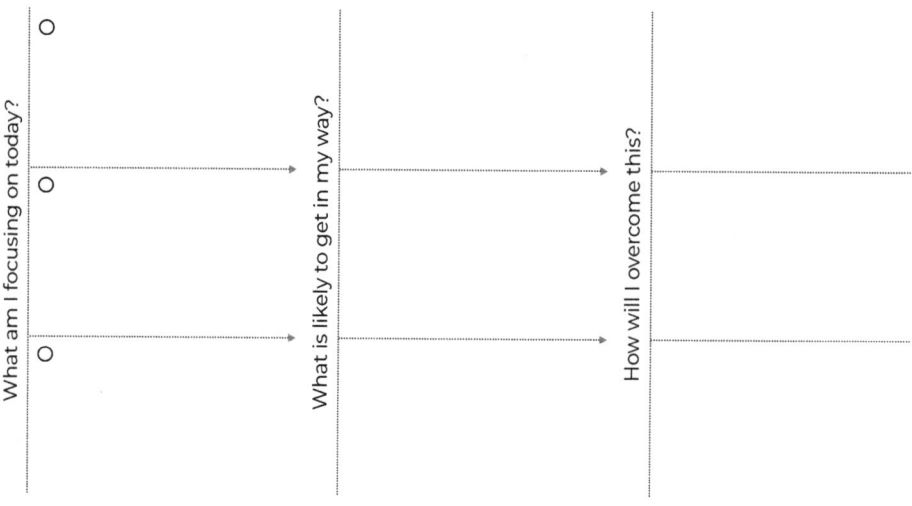

⊘ What will I say NO to today?

☾ DAILY REFLECTION

↺ What's my favorite memory from today?

✓ Did I do what I said I would do?
What can I learn from this?

○ I reviewed my weekly tasks   TODAY'S DATE ..../........../..........

♥ I am grateful for:
Because:

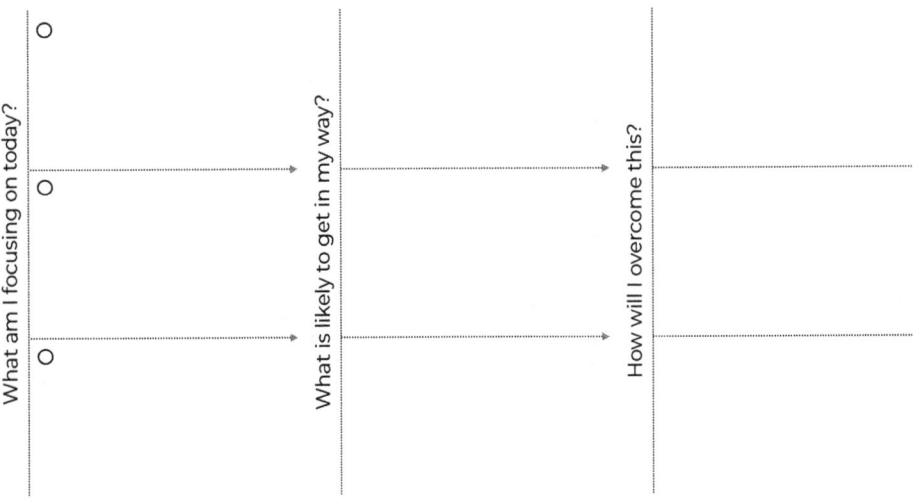

☀ **HOW CAN I GET A LITTLE CLOSER TO MY GOALS TODAY?**

🚫 What will I say NO to today?

☾ **DAILY REFLECTION**

🕘 What's my favorite memory from today?

✓ Did I do what I said I would do?
What can I learn from this?

○ I reviewed my weekly tasks   TODAY'S DATE _____/_____/_____

♥ I am grateful for:
Because:

☀ **HOW CAN I GET A LITTLE CLOSER TO MY GOALS TODAY?**

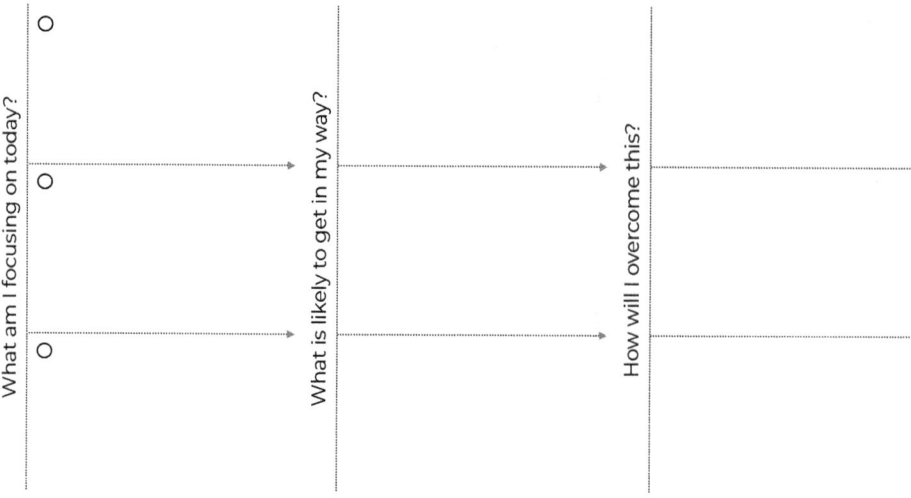

🚫 What will I say NO to today?

☾ **DAILY REFLECTION**

🕓 What's my favorite memory from today?

✓ Did I do what I said I would do?
What can I learn from this?

○ I reviewed my weekly tasks   TODAY'S DATE ..../........../..........

♥ I am grateful for:
Because:

☀ **HOW CAN I GET A LITTLE CLOSER TO MY GOALS TODAY?**

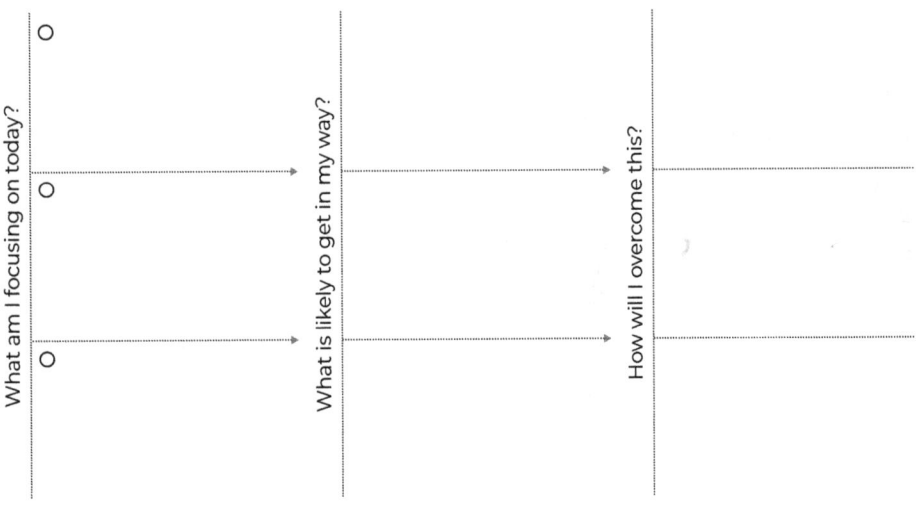

🚫 What will I say NO to today?

___

🌙 **DAILY REFLECTION**

🕐 What's my favorite memory from today?

✅ Did I do what I said I would do?
What can I learn from this?

○ I reviewed my weekly tasks   TODAY'S DATE ..../........./.........

♥ I am grateful for:
Because:

☀ **HOW CAN I GET A LITTLE CLOSER TO MY GOALS TODAY?**

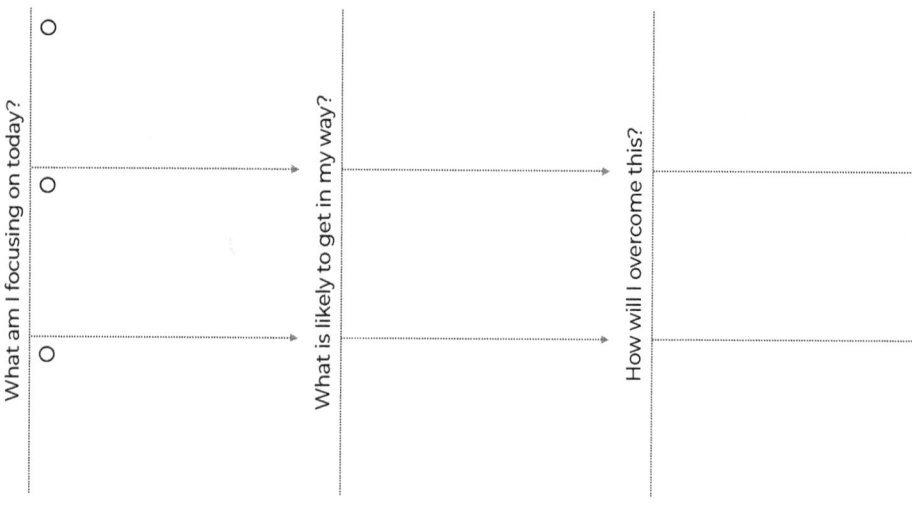

🚫 What will I say NO to today?

☾ **DAILY REFLECTION**

🕑 What's my favorite memory from today?

✔ Did I do what I said I would do?
What can I learn from this?

○ I reviewed my weekly tasks   TODAY'S DATE ..../.........../...........

♥ I am grateful for:
Because:

☀ **HOW CAN I GET A LITTLE CLOSER TO MY GOALS TODAY?**

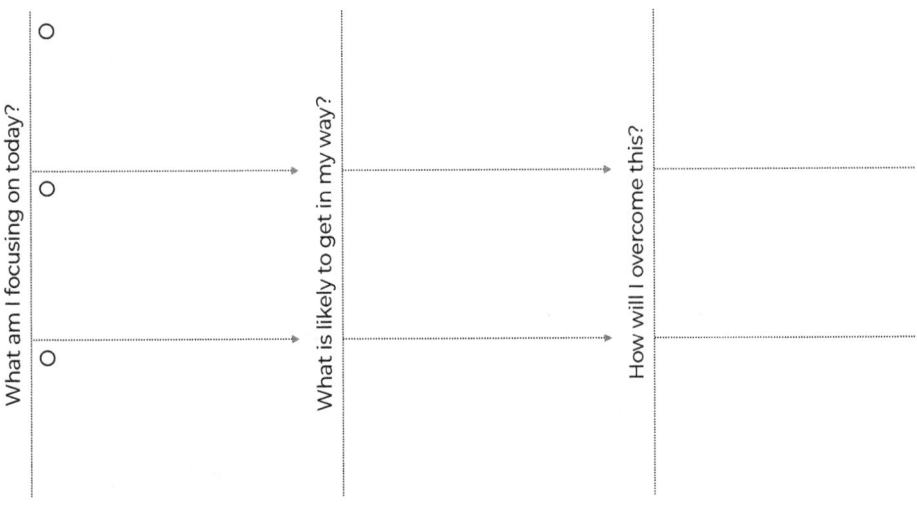

⊘ What will I say NO to today?

☾ **DAILY REFLECTION**

↻ What's my favorite memory from today?

✓ Did I do what I said I would do?
What can I learn from this?

○ I reviewed my weekly tasks

TODAY'S DATE ..../........./.........

♥ I am grateful for:
Because:

☀ HOW CAN I GET A LITTLE CLOSER TO MY GOALS TODAY?

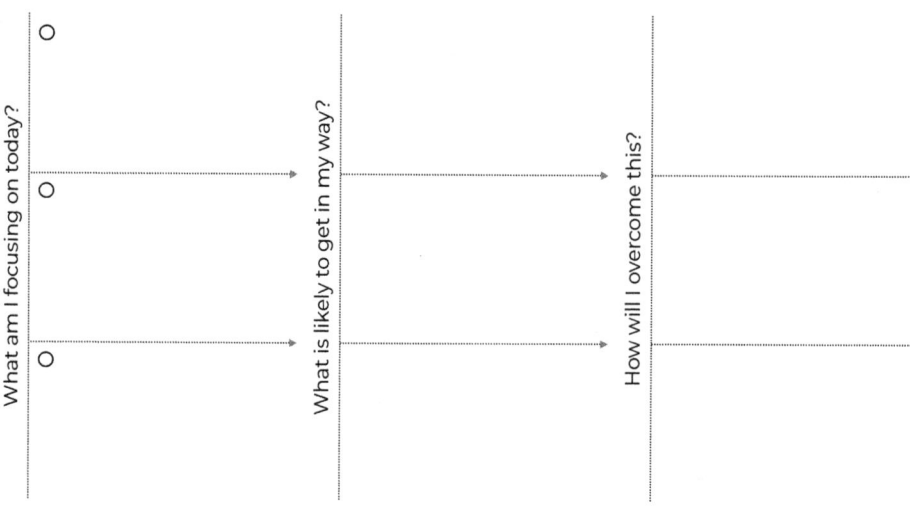

🚫 What will I say NO to today?

☾ DAILY REFLECTION

🕘 What's my favorite memory from today?

✅ Did I do what I said I would do?
What can I learn from this?

○ I reviewed my weekly tasks   TODAY'S DATE ..../........../..........

♥ I am grateful for:
Because:

☼ **HOW CAN I GET A LITTLE CLOSER TO MY GOALS TODAY?**

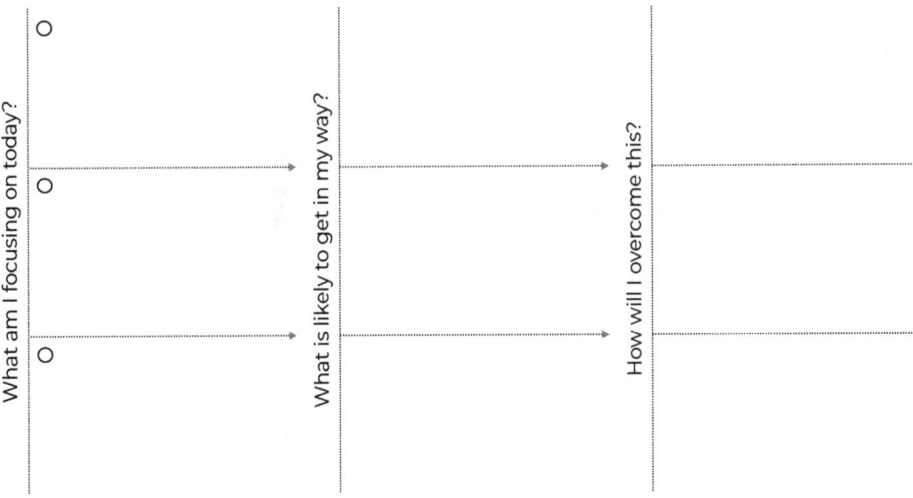

⊘ What will I say NO to today?

___

☾ **DAILY REFLECTION**

↻ What's my favorite memory from today?

✓ Did I do what I said I would do?
What can I learn from this?

○ I reviewed my weekly tasks

TODAY'S DATE ..../........../..........

♥ I am grateful for:
Because:

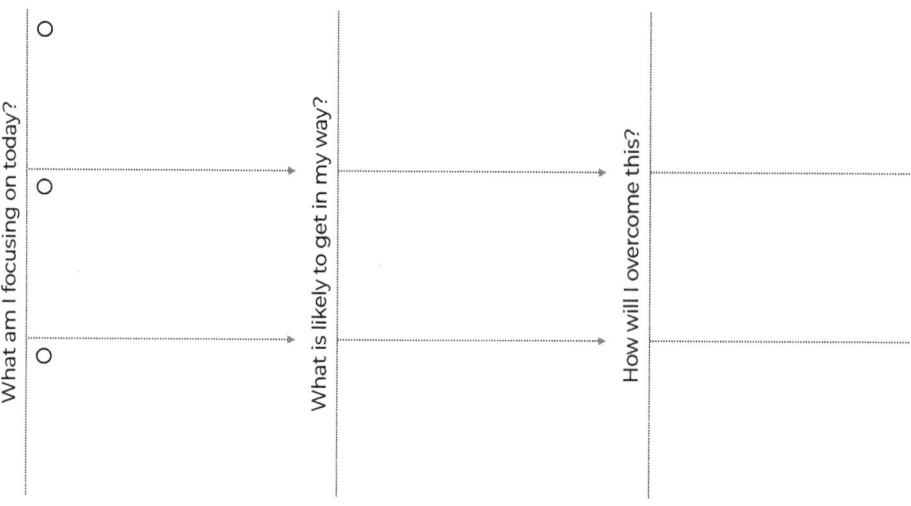

☀ **HOW CAN I GET A LITTLE CLOSER TO MY GOALS TODAY?**

⊘ What will I say NO to today?

☾ **DAILY REFLECTION**

⟲ What's my favorite memory from today?

✓ Did I do what I said I would do?
What can I learn from this?

○ I reviewed my weekly tasks   **TODAY'S DATE** _____ / _____ / _____

♥ I am grateful for:
Because:

☼ **HOW CAN I GET A LITTLE CLOSER TO MY GOALS TODAY?**

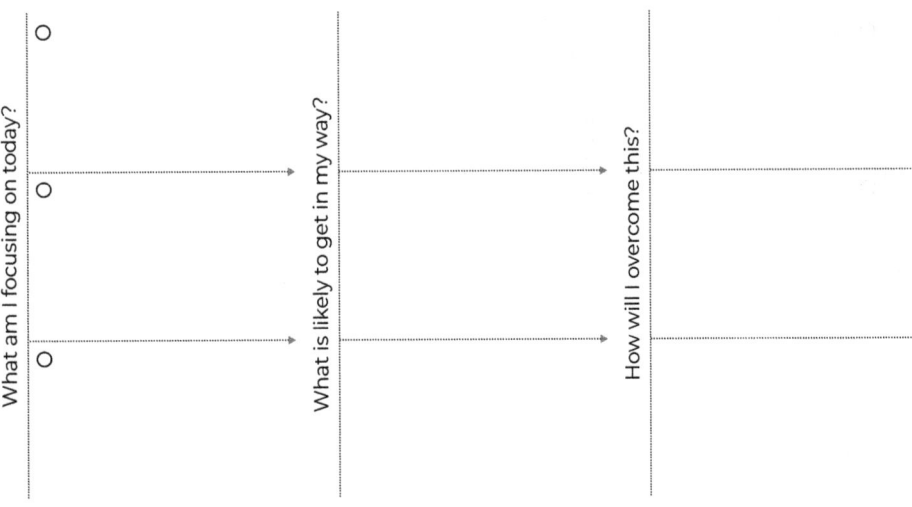

🚫 What will I say NO to today?

_____

☾ **DAILY REFLECTION**

🕘 What's my favorite memory from today?

✓ Did I do what I said I would do?
What can I learn from this?

○ I reviewed my weekly tasks   TODAY'S DATE ..../......../

♥ I am grateful for:
Because:

☀ HOW CAN I GET A LITTLE CLOSER TO MY GOALS TODAY?

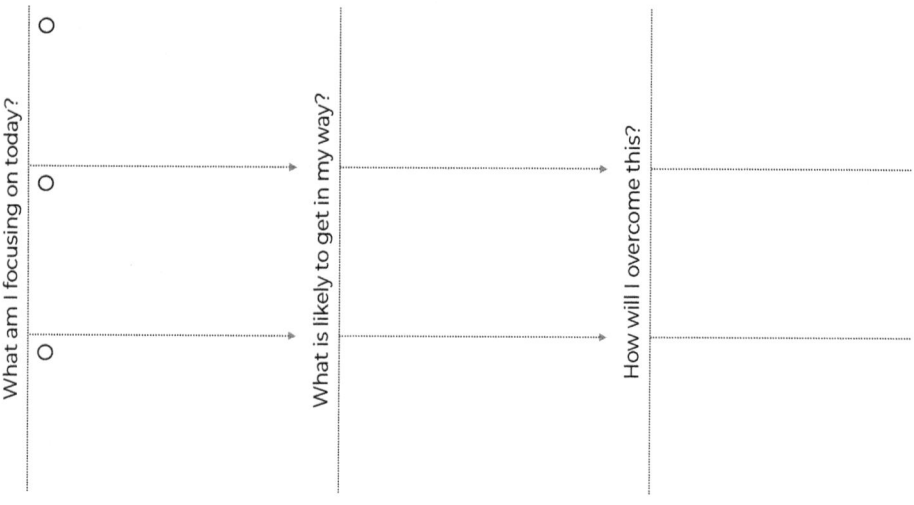

⊘ What will I say NO to today?

☾ DAILY REFLECTION

🕗 What's my favorite memory from today?

✓ Did I do what I said I would do?
What can I learn from this?

○ I reviewed my weekly tasks   TODAY'S DATE _____/_____/_____

♥ I am grateful for:
Because:

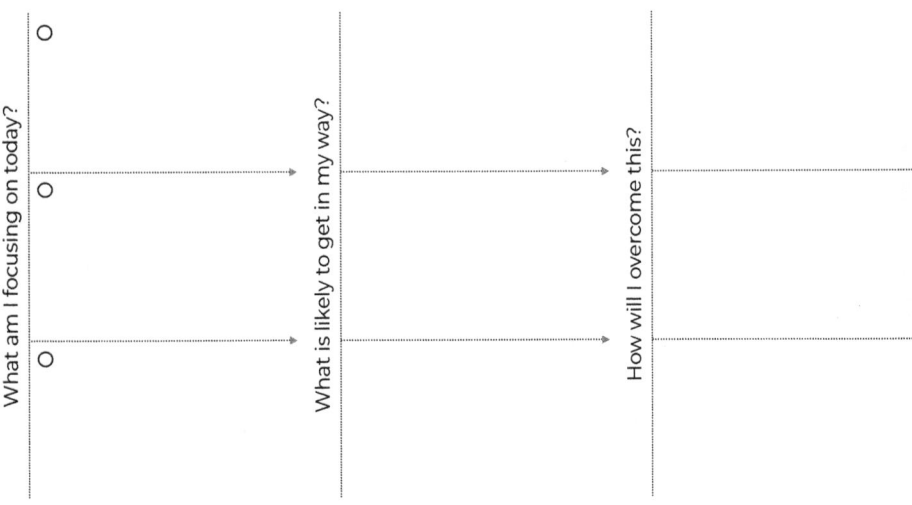

☼ **HOW CAN I GET A LITTLE CLOSER TO MY GOALS TODAY?**

⊘ What will I say NO to today?

☾ **DAILY REFLECTION**

↻ What's my favorite memory from today?

✓ Did I do what I said I would do?
What can I learn from this?

○ I reviewed my weekly tasks   TODAY'S DATE ..../........../..........

♥ I am grateful for:
Because:

☼ **HOW CAN I GET A LITTLE CLOSER TO MY GOALS TODAY?**

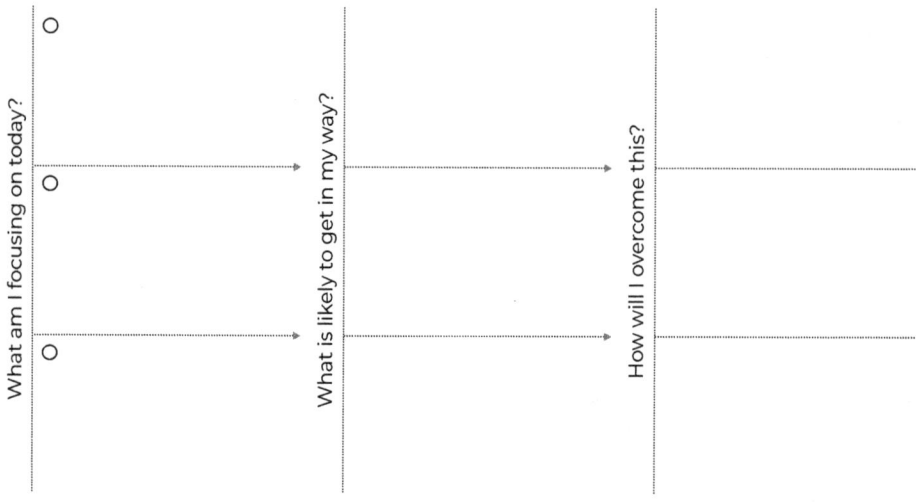

⊘ What will I say NO to today?

☾ **DAILY REFLECTION**

↻ What's my favorite memory from today?

✓ Did I do what I said I would do?
What can I learn from this?

○ I reviewed my weekly tasks   TODAY'S DATE _____/_____/_____

♥ I am grateful for:
Because:

☀ **HOW CAN I GET A LITTLE CLOSER TO MY GOALS TODAY?**

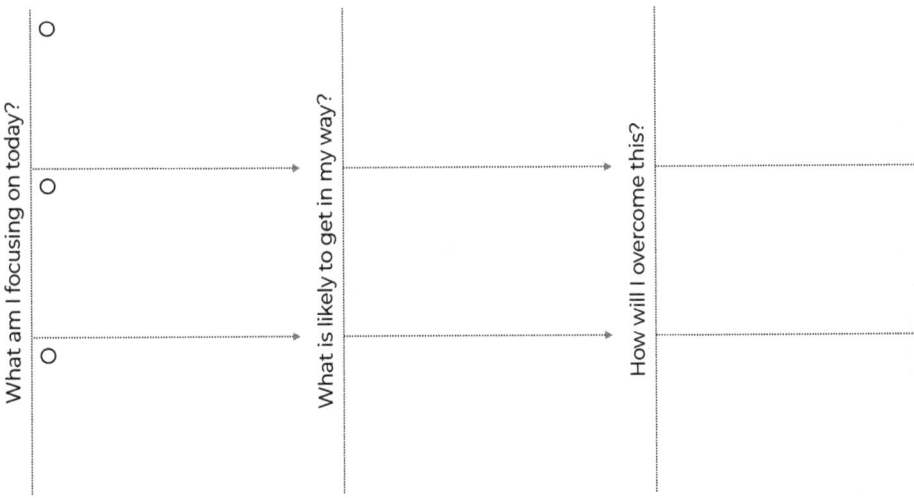

🚫 What will I say NO to today?

🌙 **DAILY REFLECTION**

🕗 What's my favorite memory from today?

✓ Did I do what I said I would do?
What can I learn from this?

○ I reviewed my weekly tasks   TODAY'S DATE _____/_____/_____

♥ I am grateful for:
Because:

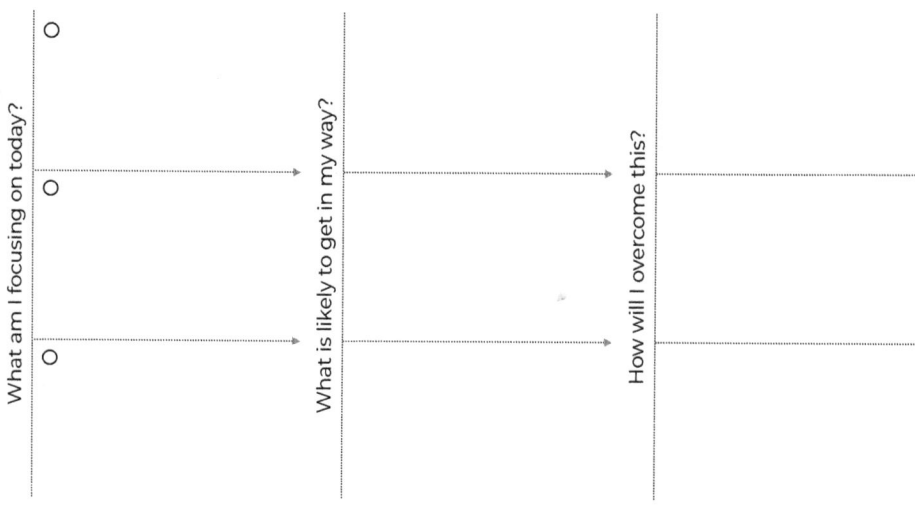

☀ HOW CAN I GET A LITTLE CLOSER TO MY GOALS TODAY?

What am I focusing on today?
○
○
○

What is likely to get in my way?

How will I overcome this?

⊘ What will I say NO to today?

☾ DAILY REFLECTION

⟲ What's my favorite memory from today?

✓ Did I do what I said I would do?
What can I learn from this?

○ I reviewed my weekly tasks

TODAY'S DATE ..../........./.........

♥ I am grateful for:

Because:

☼ **HOW CAN I GET A LITTLE CLOSER TO MY GOALS TODAY?**

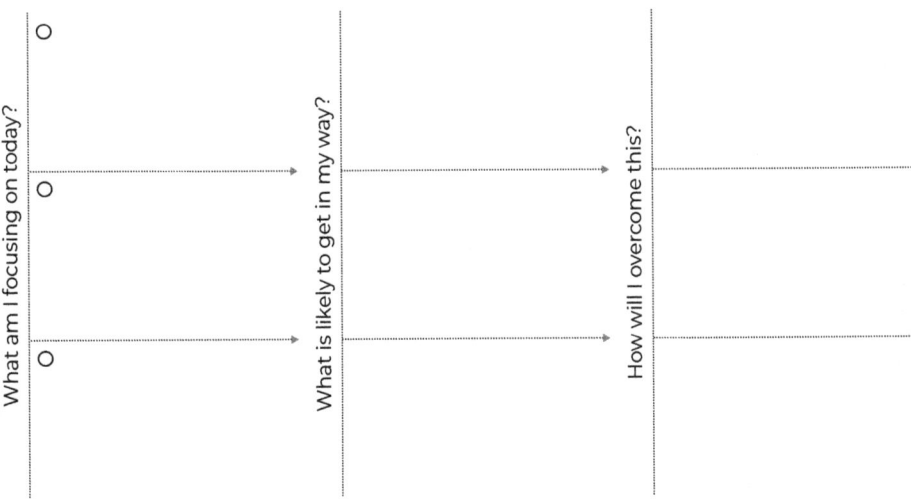

🚫 What will I say NO to today?

☾ **DAILY REFLECTION**

🕘 What's my favorite memory from today?

✓ Did I do what I said I would do?
What can I learn from this?

○ I reviewed my weekly tasks   TODAY'S DATE ..../........./.........

♥ I am grateful for:
Because:

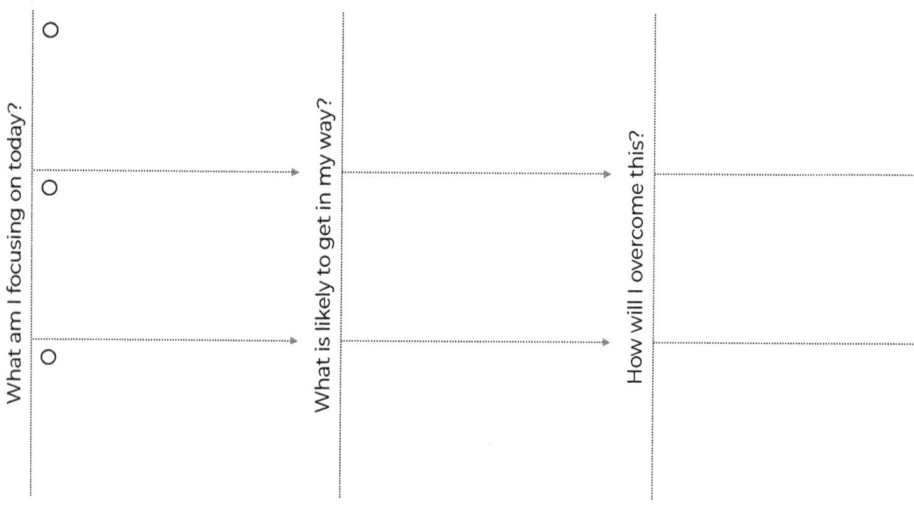

☀ **HOW CAN I GET A LITTLE CLOSER TO MY GOALS TODAY?**

What am I focusing on today?

What is likely to get in my way?

How will I overcome this?

⊘ What will I say NO to today?

☾ **DAILY REFLECTION**

🕘 What's my favorite memory from today?

✓ Did I do what I said I would do?
What can I learn from this?

○ I reviewed my weekly tasks   TODAY'S DATE _____/_____/_____

♥ I am grateful for:
Because:

☀ **HOW CAN I GET A LITTLE CLOSER TO MY GOALS TODAY?**

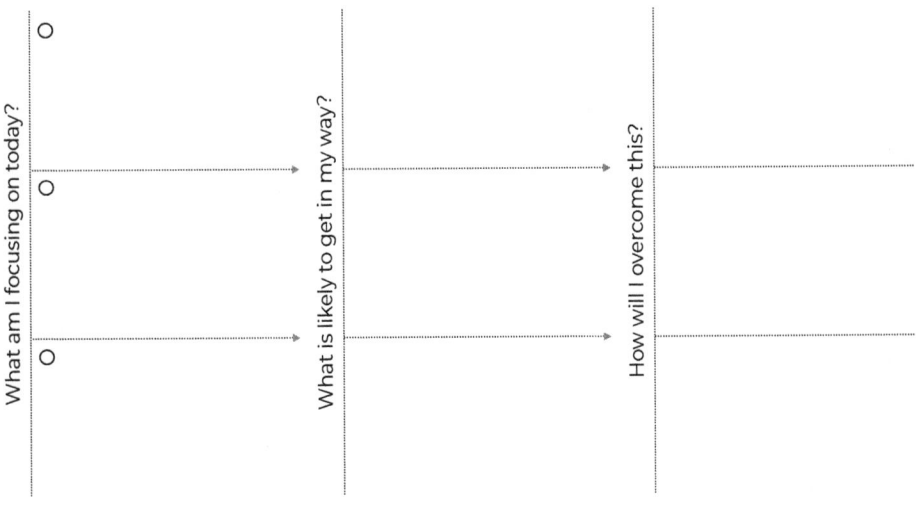

🚫 What will I say NO to today?

☾ **DAILY REFLECTION**

🕘 What's my favorite memory from today?

✅ Did I do what I said I would do?
What can I learn from this?

○ I reviewed my weekly tasks   TODAY'S DATE ..../........./.........

♥ I am grateful for:
Because:

☀ HOW CAN I GET A LITTLE CLOSER TO MY GOALS TODAY?

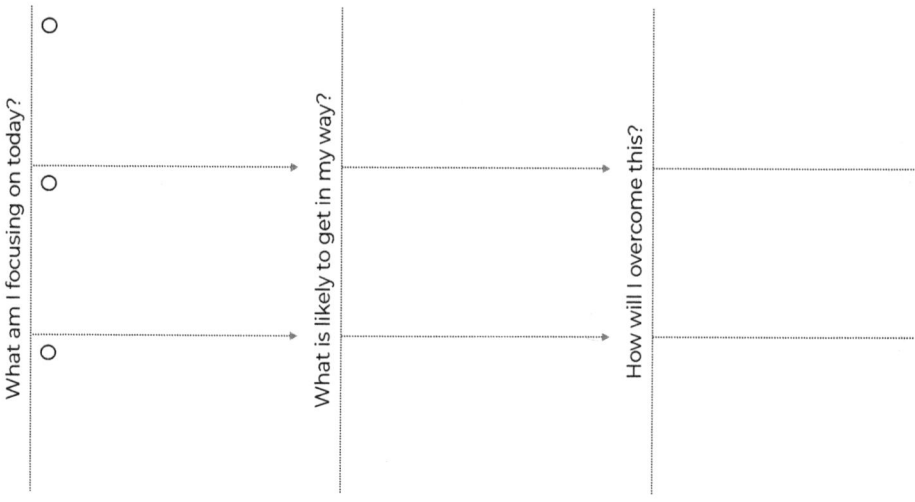

🚫 What will I say NO to today?

🌙 DAILY REFLECTION

🕓 What's my favorite memory from today?

✅ Did I do what I said I would do?
What can I learn from this?

○ I reviewed my weekly tasks

TODAY'S DATE ..../........./.........

♥ I am grateful for:
Because:

☼ HOW CAN I GET A LITTLE CLOSER TO MY GOALS TODAY?

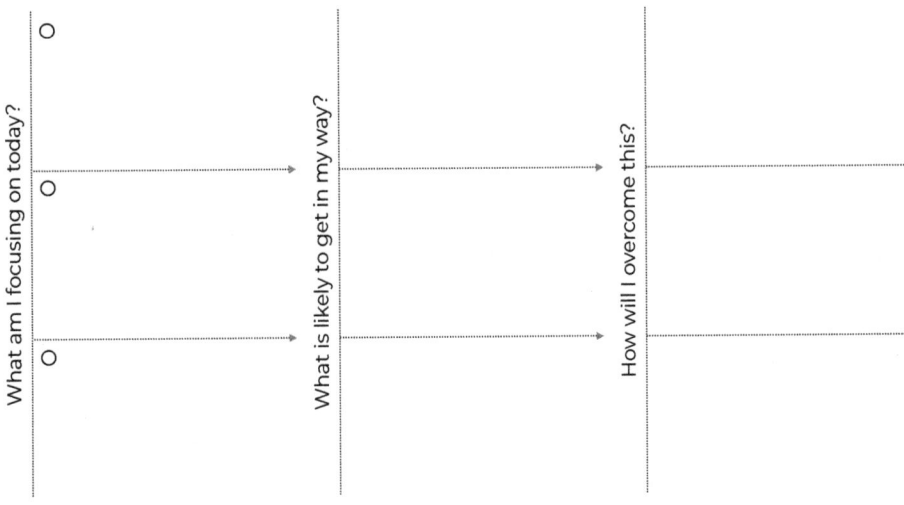

🚫 What will I say NO to today?

☾ DAILY REFLECTION

🕓 What's my favorite memory from today?

✓ Did I do what I said I would do?
What can I learn from this?

○ I reviewed my weekly tasks **TODAY'S DATE** .... / .... / ....

♥ I am grateful for:
Because:

☼ **HOW CAN I GET A LITTLE CLOSER TO MY GOALS TODAY?**

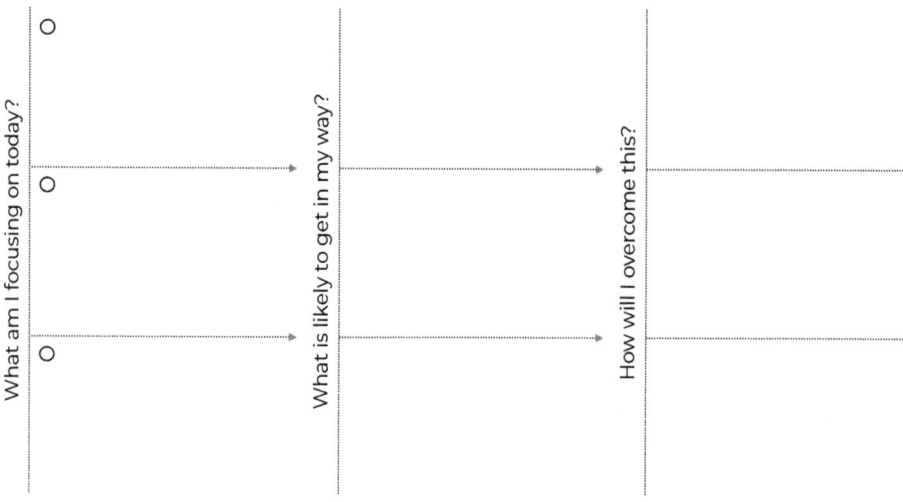

🚫 What will I say NO to today?

☾ **DAILY REFLECTION**

🕒 What's my favorite memory from today?

✅ Did I do what I said I would do?
What can I learn from this?

○ I reviewed my weekly tasks   TODAY'S DATE ..../........../..........

♥ I am grateful for:
Because:

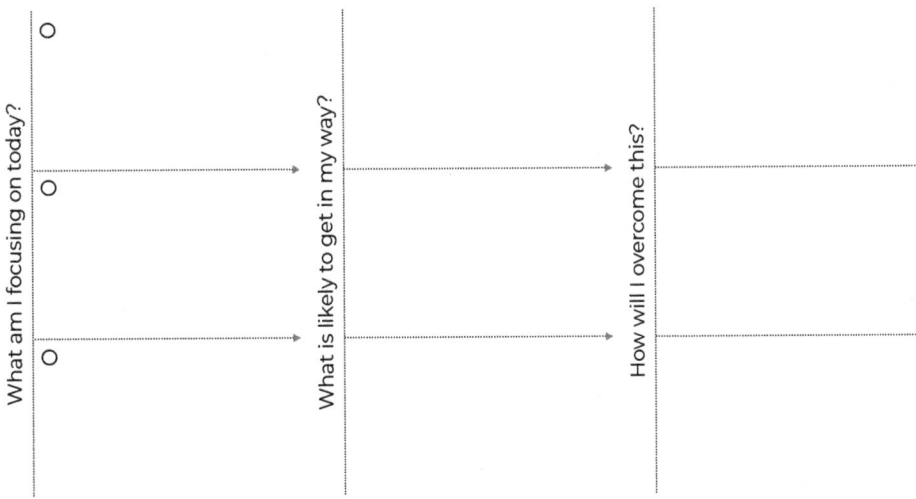

☀ HOW CAN I GET A LITTLE CLOSER TO MY GOALS TODAY?

🚫 What will I say NO to today?

_____

☾ DAILY REFLECTION

🕚 What's my favorite memory from today?

✅ Did I do what I said I would do?
What can I learn from this?

○ I reviewed my weekly tasks   TODAY'S DATE .... / .... / ....

♥ I am grateful for:
Because:

☼ HOW CAN I GET A LITTLE CLOSER TO MY GOALS TODAY?

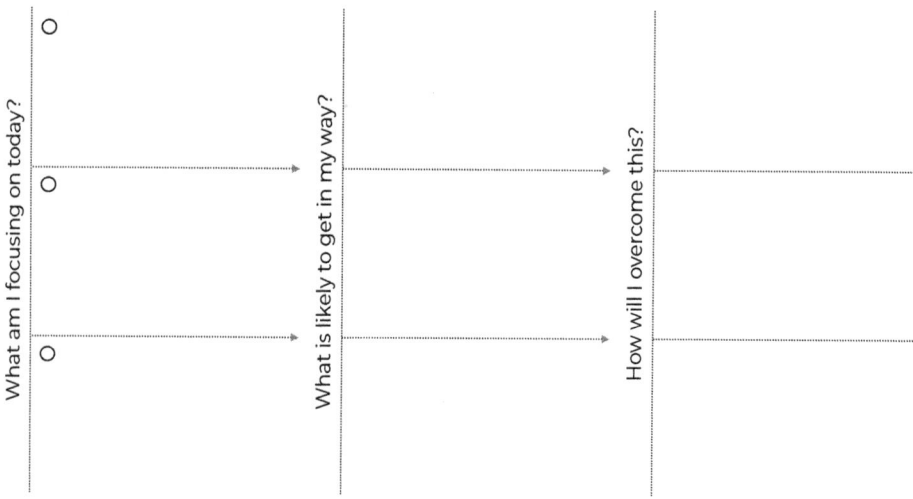

⊘ What will I say NO to today?

☾ DAILY REFLECTION

⏳ What's my favorite memory from today?

✓ Did I do what I said I would do?
What can I learn from this?

○ I reviewed my weekly tasks   TODAY'S DATE _____/_____/_____

♥ I am grateful for:
Because:

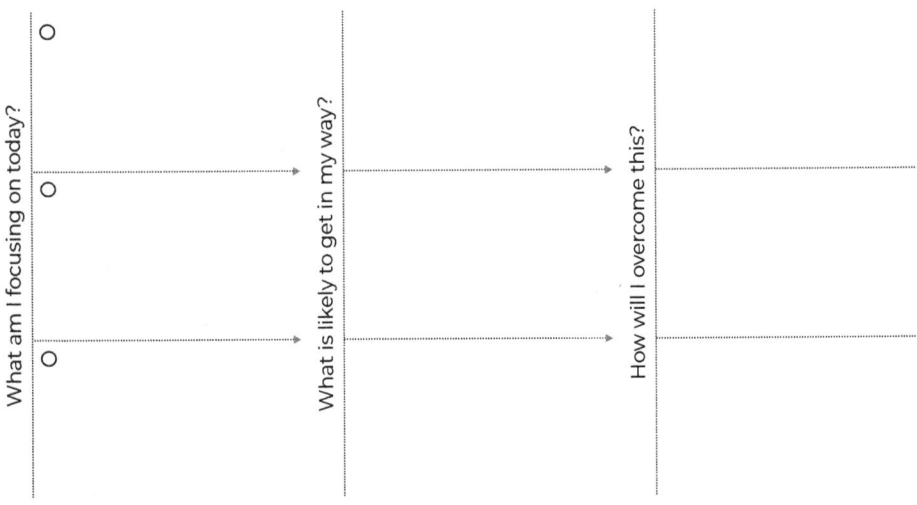

☀ **HOW CAN I GET A LITTLE CLOSER TO MY GOALS TODAY?**

⃠ What will I say NO to today?

_____

☾ **DAILY REFLECTION**

🕗 What's my favorite memory from today?

✓ Did I do what I said I would do?
What can I learn from this?

○ I reviewed my weekly tasks   TODAY'S DATE ..../........./.........

♥ I am grateful for:
Because:

☀ **HOW CAN I GET A LITTLE CLOSER TO MY GOALS TODAY?**

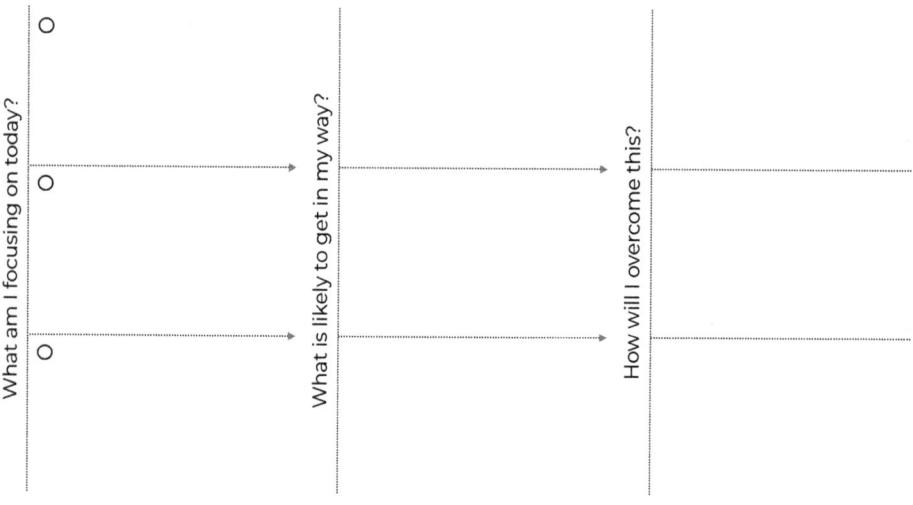

🚫 What will I say NO to today?

☾ **DAILY REFLECTION**

🕘 What's my favorite memory from today?

✅ Did I do what I said I would do?
What can I learn from this?

○ I reviewed my weekly tasks   TODAY'S DATE ..../........../..........

♥ I am grateful for:
Because:

☼ **HOW CAN I GET A LITTLE CLOSER TO MY GOALS TODAY?**

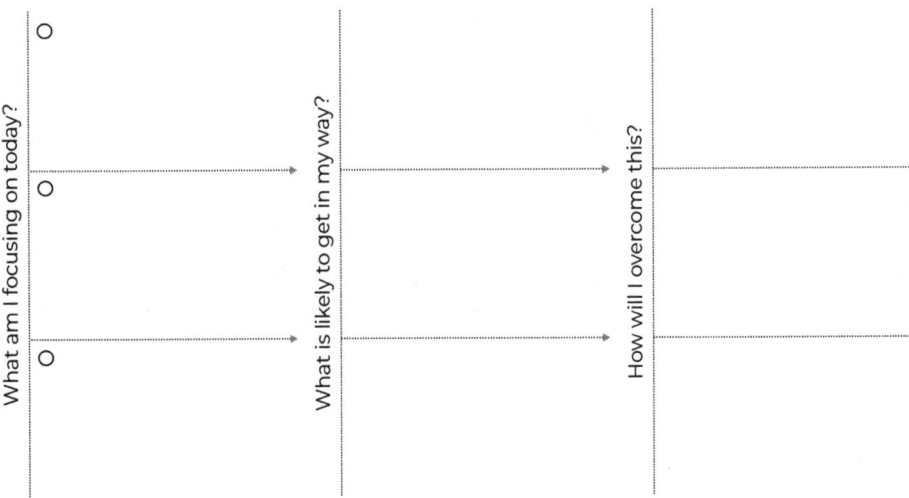

🚫 What will I say NO to today?

_____

☾ **DAILY REFLECTION**

🕗 What's my favorite memory from today?

✓ Did I do what I said I would do?
What can I learn from this?

○ I reviewed my weekly tasks   TODAY'S DATE _____ / _____ / _____

♥ I am grateful for:
Because:

☀ **HOW CAN I GET A LITTLE CLOSER TO MY GOALS TODAY?**

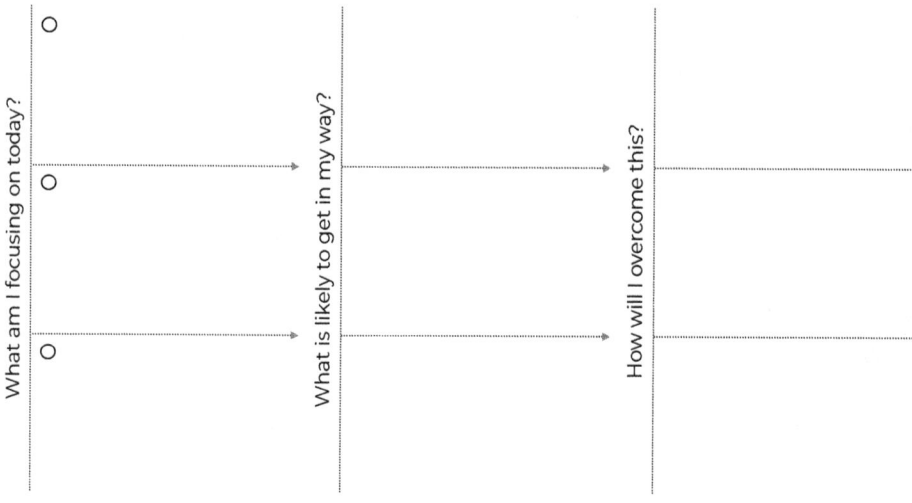

🚫 What will I say NO to today?

☾ **DAILY REFLECTION**

🕤 What's my favorite memory from today?

✅ Did I do what I said I would do?
What can I learn from this?

○ I reviewed my weekly tasks   TODAY'S DATE .... / .... / ....

♥ I am grateful for:
Because:

☀ **HOW CAN I GET A LITTLE CLOSER TO MY GOALS TODAY?**

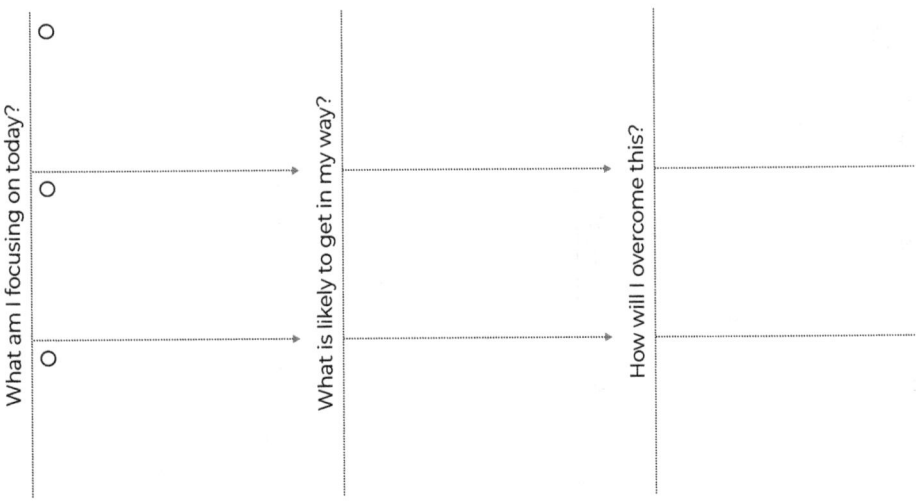

⊘ What will I say NO to today?

☾ **DAILY REFLECTION**

🕑 What's my favorite memory from today?

✓ Did I do what I said I would do?
What can I learn from this?

○ I reviewed my weekly tasks		TODAY'S DATE ..../............./.............

♥ I am grateful for:
Because:

☼ **HOW CAN I GET A LITTLE CLOSER TO MY GOALS TODAY?**

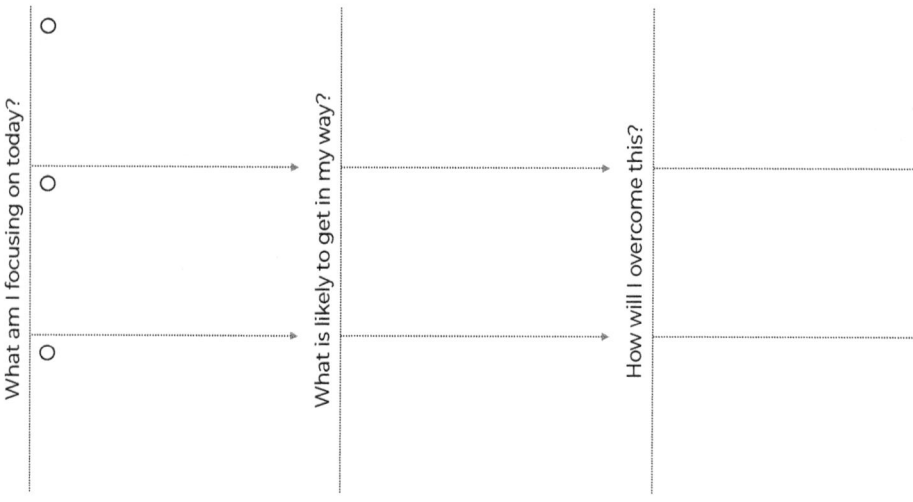

⊘ What will I say NO to today?

___

☾ **DAILY REFLECTION**

🕓 What's my favorite memory from today?

✓ Did I do what I said I would do?
What can I learn from this?

○ I reviewed my weekly tasks   TODAY'S DATE ..../........../..........

♥ I am grateful for:
Because:

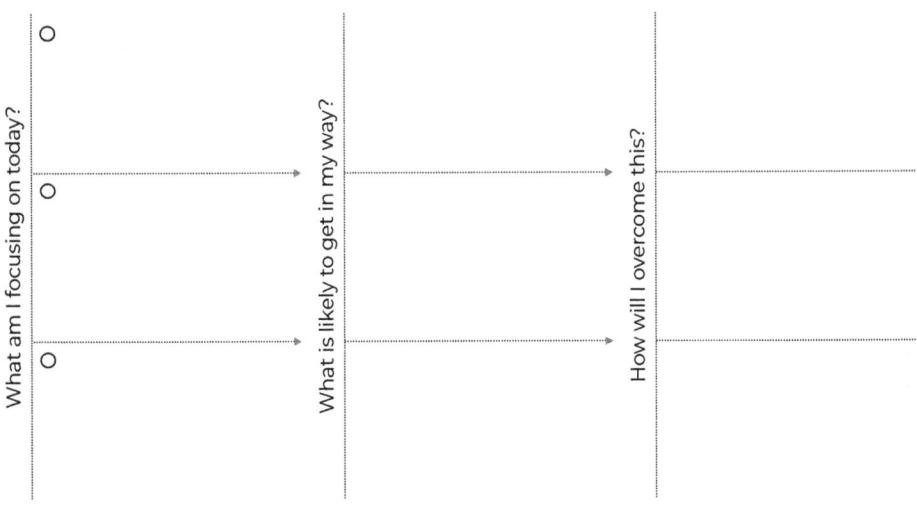

☼ **HOW CAN I GET A LITTLE CLOSER TO MY GOALS TODAY?**

⊘ What will I say NO to today?

☾ **DAILY REFLECTION**

↻ What's my favorite memory from today?

✓ Did I do what I said I would do?
What can I learn from this?

◯ I reviewed my weekly tasks   TODAY'S DATE ..../........./.........

♥ I am grateful for:
Because:

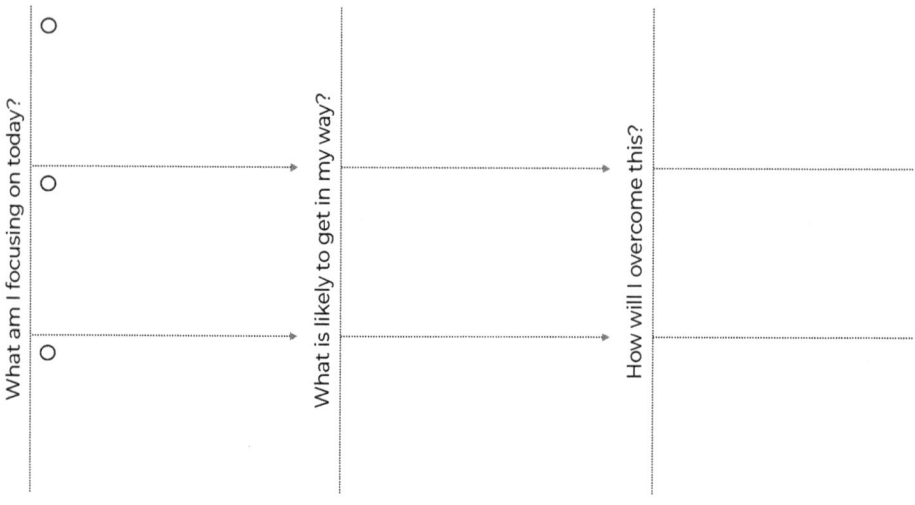

☀ HOW CAN I GET A LITTLE CLOSER TO MY GOALS TODAY?

What am I focusing on today?

What is likely to get in my way?

How will I overcome this?

⃠ What will I say NO to today?

☾ DAILY REFLECTION

🕗 What's my favorite memory from today?

✅ Did I do what I said I would do?
What can I learn from this?

○ I reviewed my weekly tasks

TODAY'S DATE _____/_____/_____

♥ I am grateful for:

Because:

☀ **HOW CAN I GET A LITTLE CLOSER TO MY GOALS TODAY?**

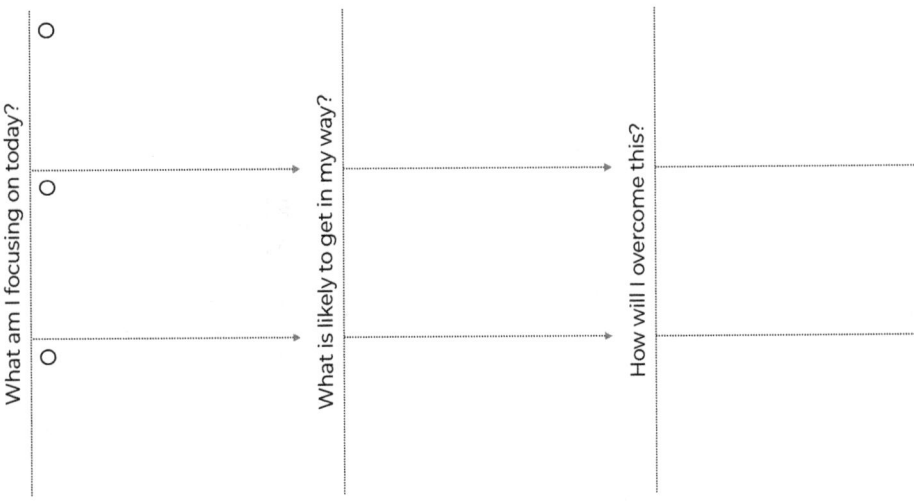

🚫 What will I say NO to today?

_____

☾ **DAILY REFLECTION**

🕘 What's my favorite memory from today?

✓ Did I do what I said I would do?
What can I learn from this?

○ I reviewed my weekly tasks

TODAY'S DATE ..../........../..........

♥ I am grateful for:
Because:

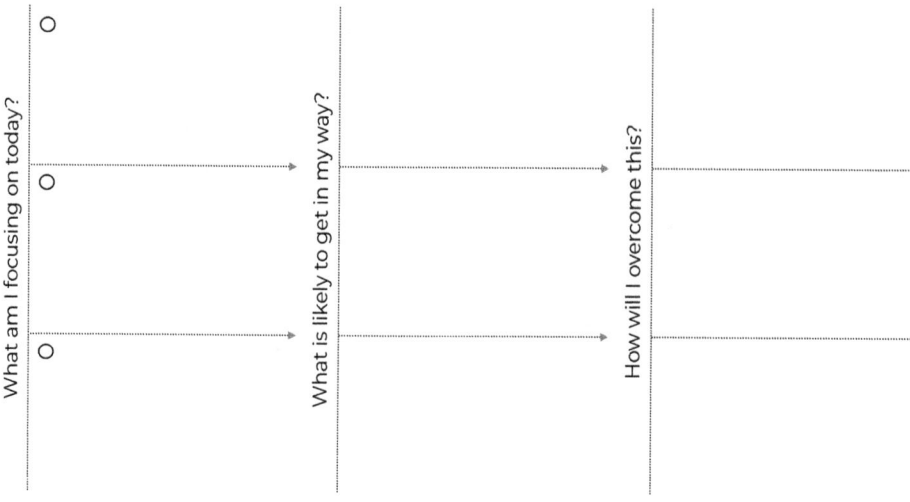

☀ **HOW CAN I GET A LITTLE CLOSER TO MY GOALS TODAY?**

🚫 What will I say NO to today?

🌙 **DAILY REFLECTION**

🕘 What's my favorite memory from today?

✅ Did I do what I said I would do?
What can I learn from this?

○ I reviewed my weekly tasks   TODAY'S DATE _____/_____/_____

♥ I am grateful for:
Because:

☀ **HOW CAN I GET A LITTLE CLOSER TO MY GOALS TODAY?**

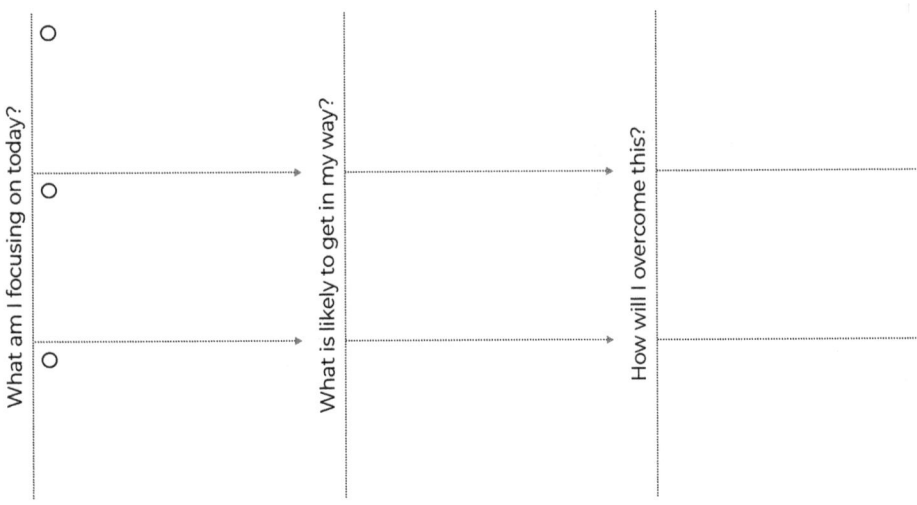

⊘ What will I say NO to today?

_____

☾ **DAILY REFLECTION**

🕒 What's my favorite memory from today?

✓ Did I do what I said I would do?
What can I learn from this?

○ I reviewed my weekly tasks   TODAY'S DATE ..../.........../...........

♥ I am grateful for:
Because:

☀ HOW CAN I GET A LITTLE CLOSER TO MY GOALS TODAY?

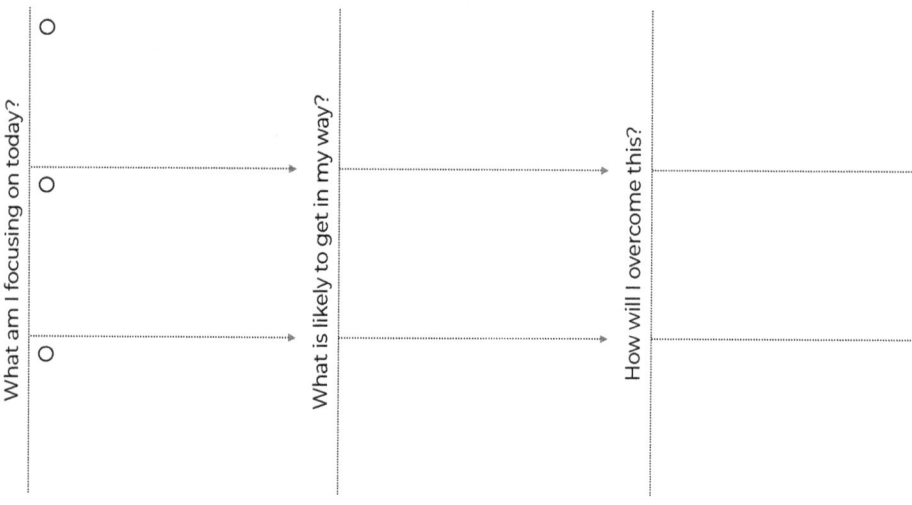

🚫 What will I say NO to today?

☾ DAILY REFLECTION

🕗 What's my favorite memory from today?

✓ Did I do what I said I would do?
What can I learn from this?

○ I reviewed my weekly tasks

TODAY'S DATE ..../........../..........

♥ I am grateful for:
Because:

☀ **HOW CAN I GET A LITTLE CLOSER TO MY GOALS TODAY?**

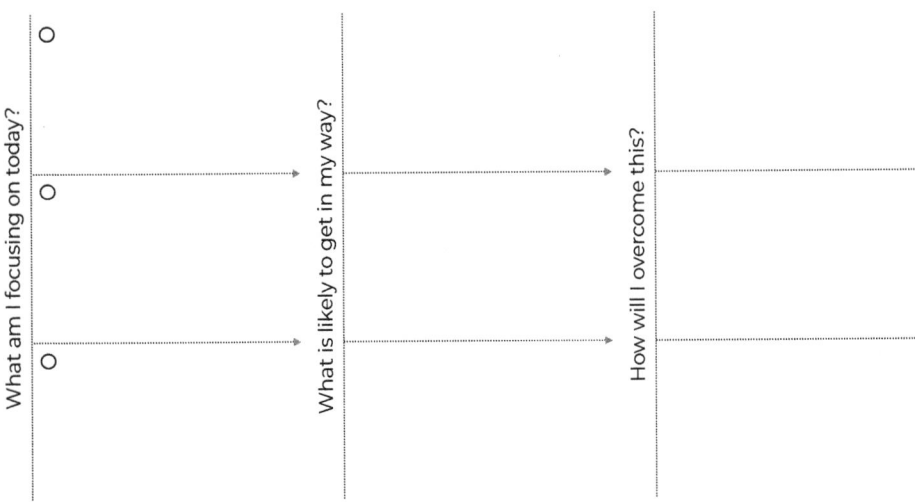

⊘ What will I say NO to today?

☾ **DAILY REFLECTION**

↻ What's my favorite memory from today?

✓ Did I do what I said I would do?
What can I learn from this?

○ I reviewed my weekly tasks

TODAY'S DATE ..../........../..........

♥ I am grateful for:
Because:

☀ HOW CAN I GET A LITTLE CLOSER TO MY GOALS TODAY?

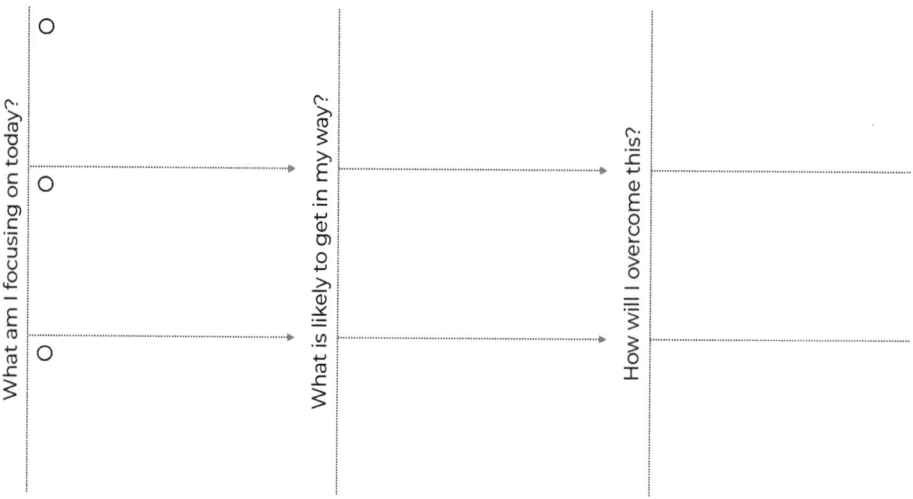

⊘ What will I say NO to today?

☾ DAILY REFLECTION

🕘 What's my favorite memory from today?

✓ Did I do what I said I would do?
What can I learn from this?

○ I reviewed my weekly tasks   TODAY'S DATE ..../.........../..........

♥ I am grateful for:
Because:

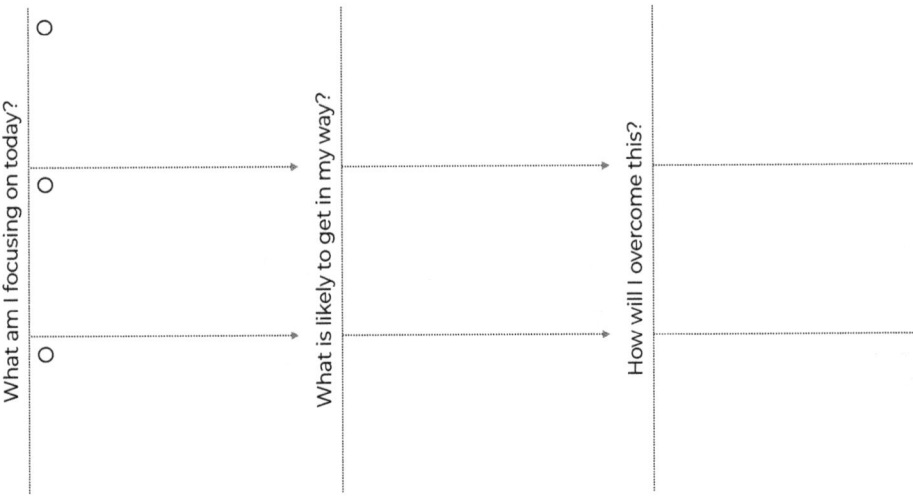

☼ **HOW CAN I GET A LITTLE CLOSER TO MY GOALS TODAY?**

⊘ What will I say NO to today?

☾ **DAILY REFLECTION**

⟲ What's my favorite memory from today?

✓ Did I do what I said I would do?
What can I learn from this?

○ I reviewed my weekly tasks   TODAY'S DATE ..../.........../...........

♥ I am grateful for:
Because:

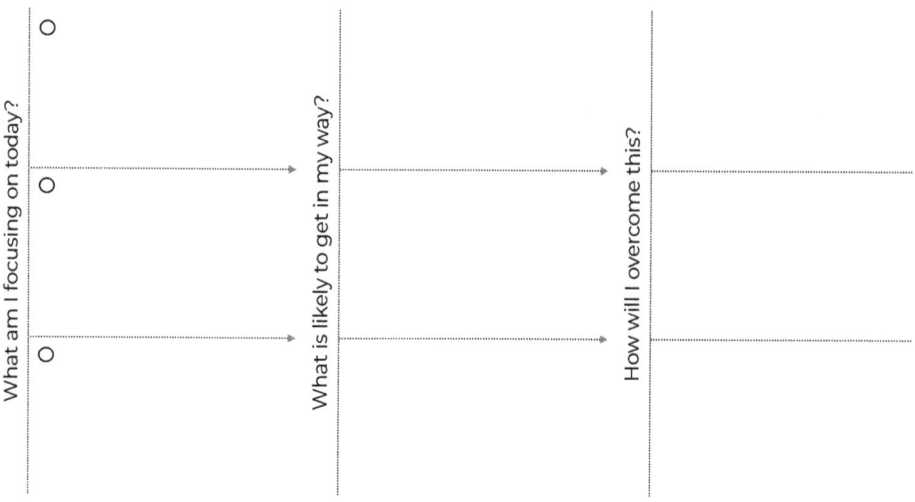

☀ HOW CAN I GET A LITTLE CLOSER TO MY GOALS TODAY?

⊘ What will I say NO to today?

☾ DAILY REFLECTION

🕘 What's my favorite memory from today?

✓ Did I do what I said I would do?
What can I learn from this?

○ I reviewed my weekly tasks   TODAY'S DATE _____ /_____ /_____

♥ I am grateful for:
Because:

☀ **HOW CAN I GET A LITTLE CLOSER TO MY GOALS TODAY?**

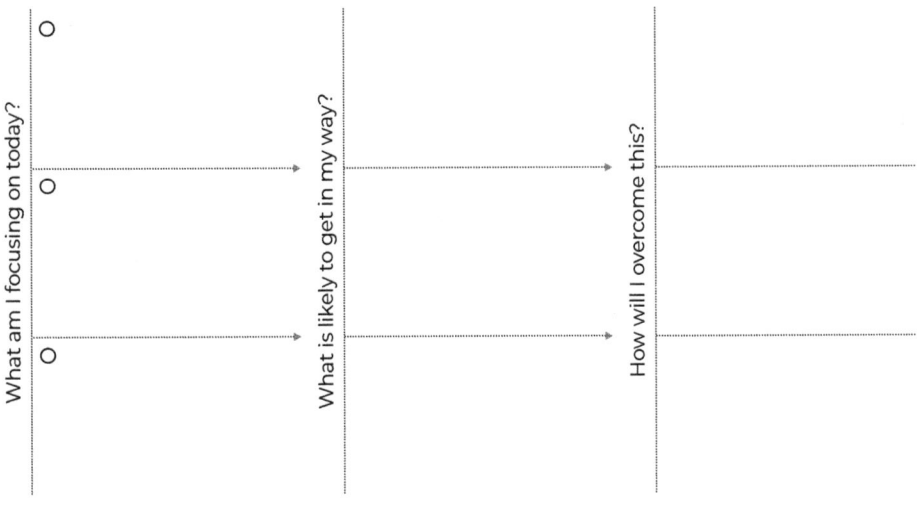

🚫 What will I say NO to today?

_____

☾ **DAILY REFLECTION**

🕗 What's my favorite memory from today?

✅ Did I do what I said I would do?
What can I learn from this?

○ I reviewed my weekly tasks   TODAY'S DATE _____/_____/_____

♥ I am grateful for:
Because:

☀ HOW CAN I GET A LITTLE CLOSER TO MY GOALS TODAY?

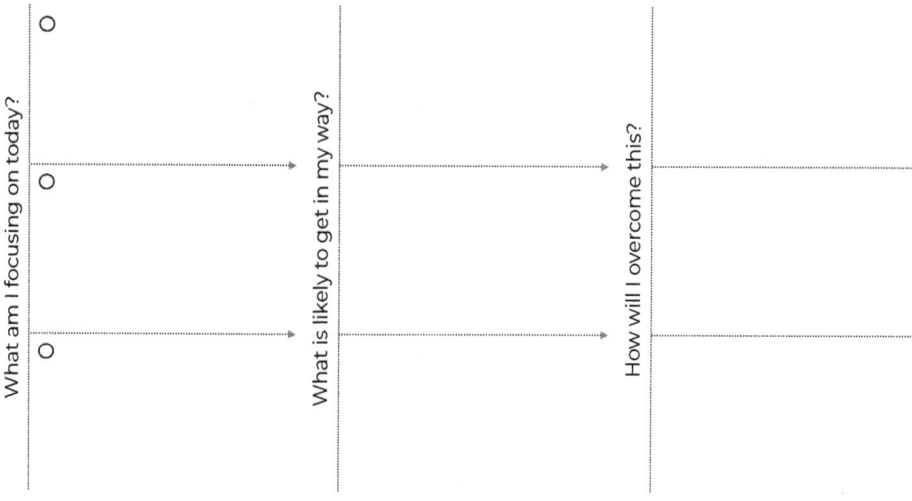

🚫 What will I say NO to today?

☾ DAILY REFLECTION

🕗 What's my favorite memory from today?

✓ Did I do what I said I would do?
What can I learn from this?

○ I reviewed my weekly tasks   TODAY'S DATE ..../........../..........

♥ I am grateful for:
Because:

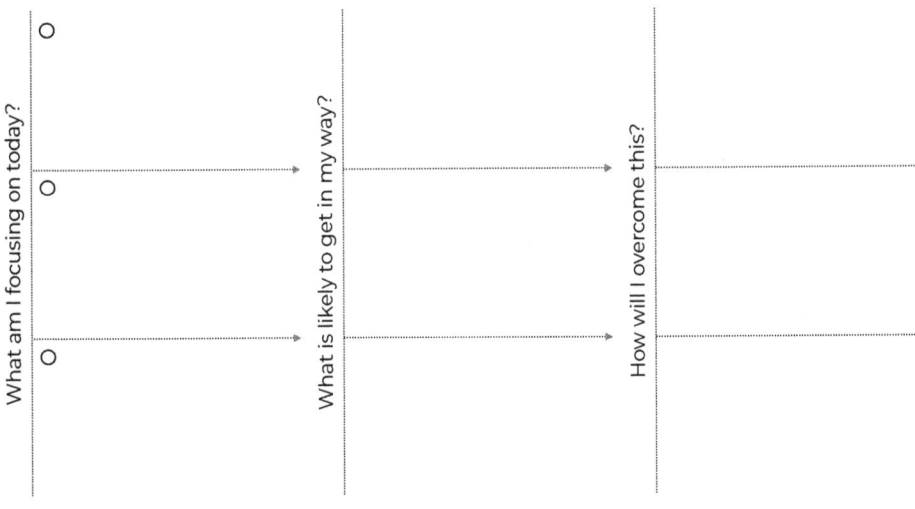

☀ **HOW CAN I GET A LITTLE CLOSER TO MY GOALS TODAY?**

🚫 What will I say NO to today?

🌙 **DAILY REFLECTION**

🕘 What's my favorite memory from today?

✓ Did I do what I said I would do?
What can I learn from this?

○ I reviewed my weekly tasks   TODAY'S DATE ..../.........../...........

♥ I am grateful for:
Because:

☀ HOW CAN I GET A LITTLE CLOSER TO MY GOALS TODAY?

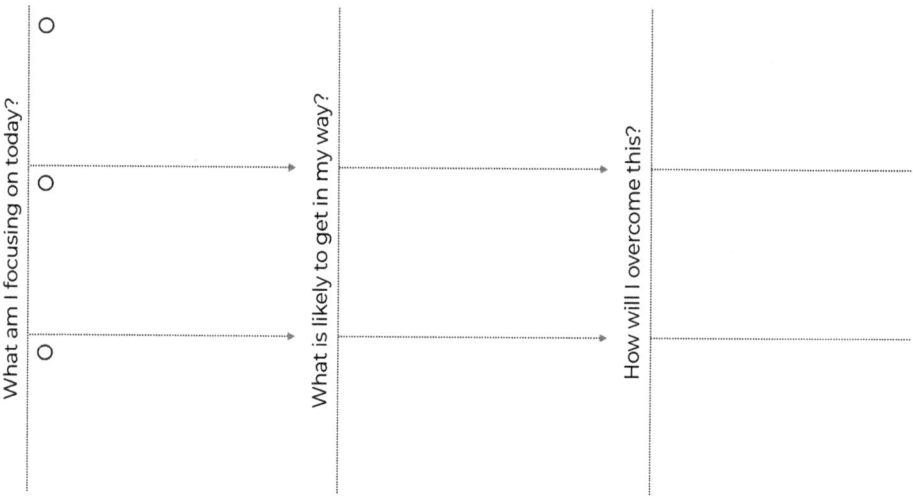

🚫 What will I say NO to today?

☾ DAILY REFLECTION

🕘 What's my favorite memory from today?

✓ Did I do what I said I would do?
What can I learn from this?

○ I reviewed my weekly tasks   TODAY'S DATE ..../........../..........

♥ I am grateful for:
Because:

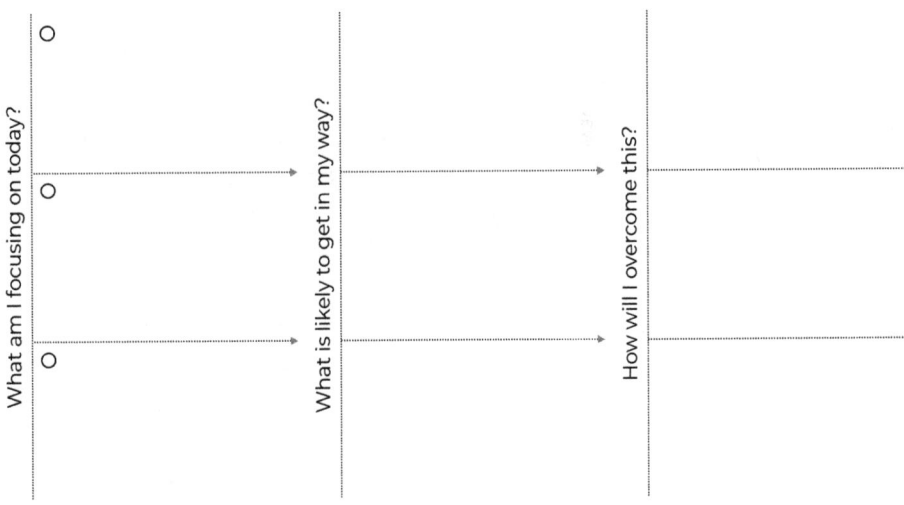

☼ **HOW CAN I GET A LITTLE CLOSER TO MY GOALS TODAY?**

⊘ What will I say NO to today?

___

☾ **DAILY REFLECTION**

↺ What's my favorite memory from today?

✓ Did I do what I said I would do?
What can I learn from this?

○ I reviewed my weekly tasks   **TODAY'S DATE** ..../......../........

♥ I am grateful for:
Because:

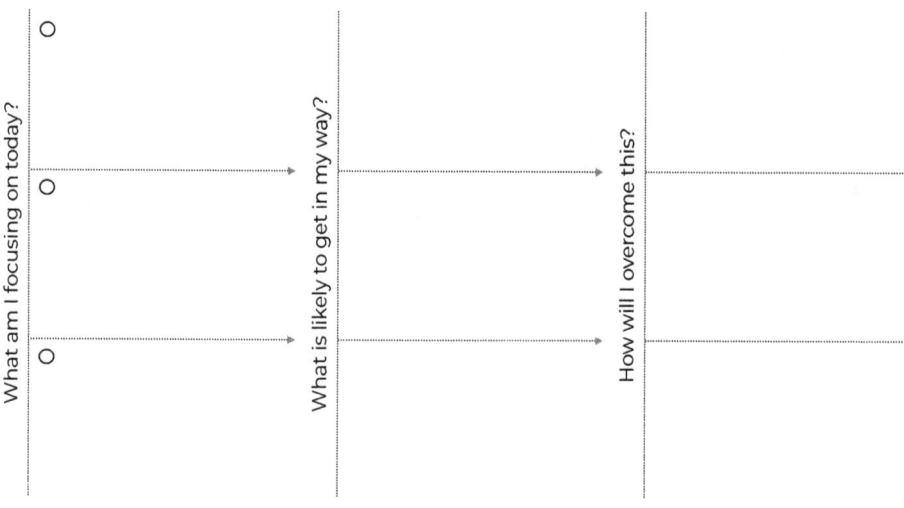

☼ **HOW CAN I GET A LITTLE CLOSER TO MY GOALS TODAY?**

⊘ What will I say NO to today?

☾ **DAILY REFLECTION**

⟲ What's my favorite memory from today?

✓ Did I do what I said I would do?
What can I learn from this?

○ I reviewed my weekly tasks TODAY'S DATE ..../........../..........

♥ I am grateful for:
Because:

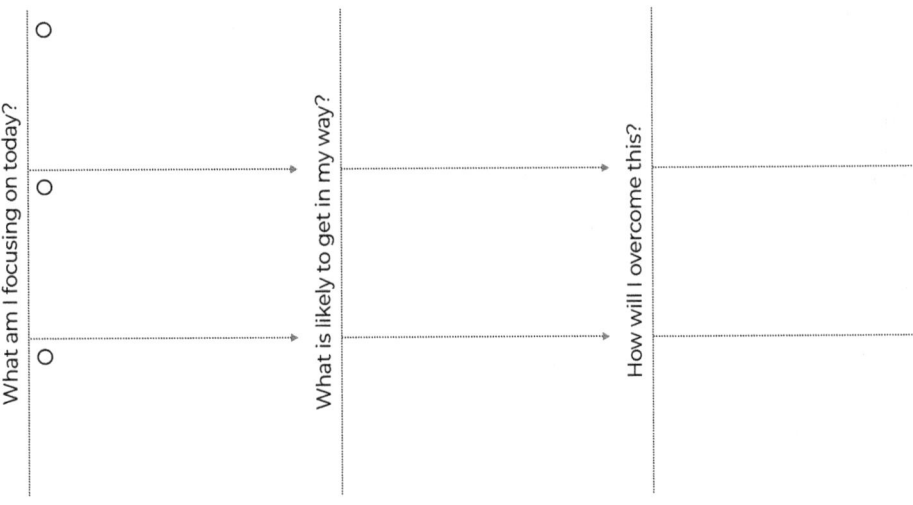

☼ **HOW CAN I GET A LITTLE CLOSER TO MY GOALS TODAY?**

⊘ What will I say NO to today?

___

☾ **DAILY REFLECTION**

🕘 What's my favorite memory from today?

✅ Did I do what I said I would do?
What can I learn from this?

○ I reviewed my weekly tasks

TODAY'S DATE ..../........../..........

♥ I am grateful for:

Because:

☀ HOW CAN I GET A LITTLE CLOSER TO MY GOALS TODAY?

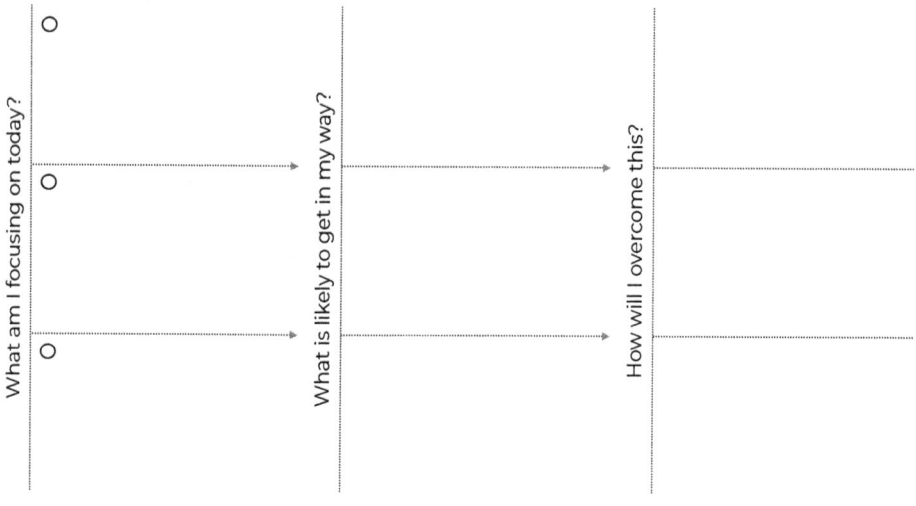

⊘ What will I say NO to today?

☾ DAILY REFLECTION

🕒 What's my favorite memory from today?

✓ Did I do what I said I would do?
What can I learn from this?

○ I reviewed my weekly tasks   TODAY'S DATE ..../........../..........

♥ I am grateful for:
Because:

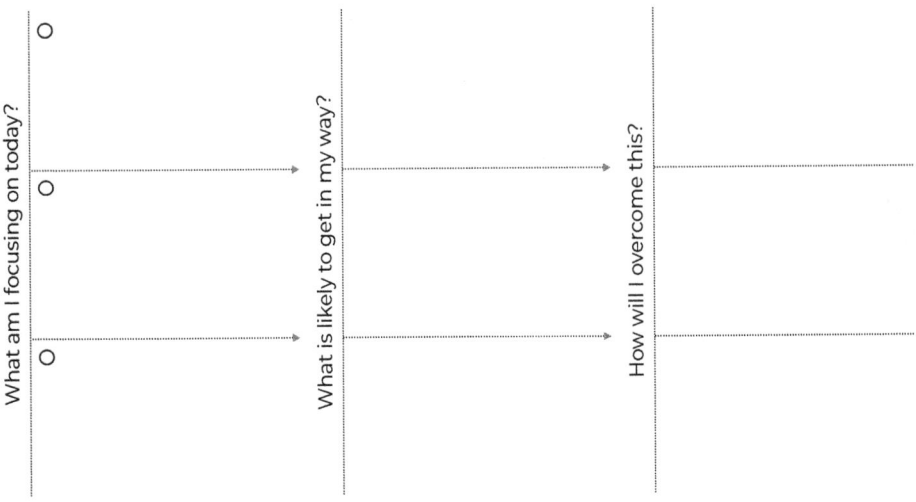

☀ **HOW CAN I GET A LITTLE CLOSER TO MY GOALS TODAY?**

⊘ What will I say NO to today?

___

☾ **DAILY REFLECTION**

⟲ What's my favorite memory from today?

✓ Did I do what I said I would do?
What can I learn from this?

○ I reviewed my weekly tasks   TODAY'S DATE ..../........../..........

♥ I am grateful for:
Because:

☼ HOW CAN I GET A LITTLE CLOSER TO MY GOALS TODAY?

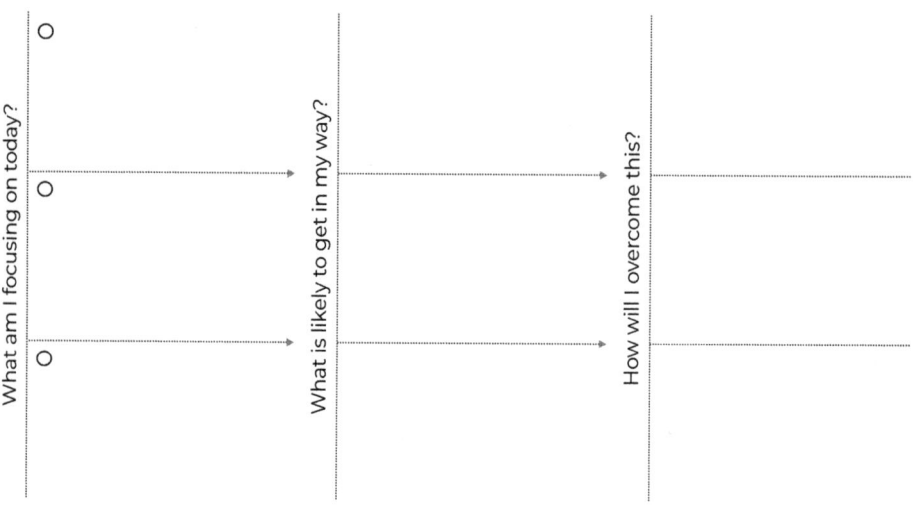

⊘ What will I say NO to today?

☾ DAILY REFLECTION

⟲ What's my favorite memory from today?

✓ Did I do what I said I would do?
What can I learn from this?

○ I reviewed my weekly tasks   TODAY'S DATE ..../........./.........

♥ I am grateful for:
Because:

☀ HOW CAN I GET A LITTLE CLOSER TO MY GOALS TODAY?

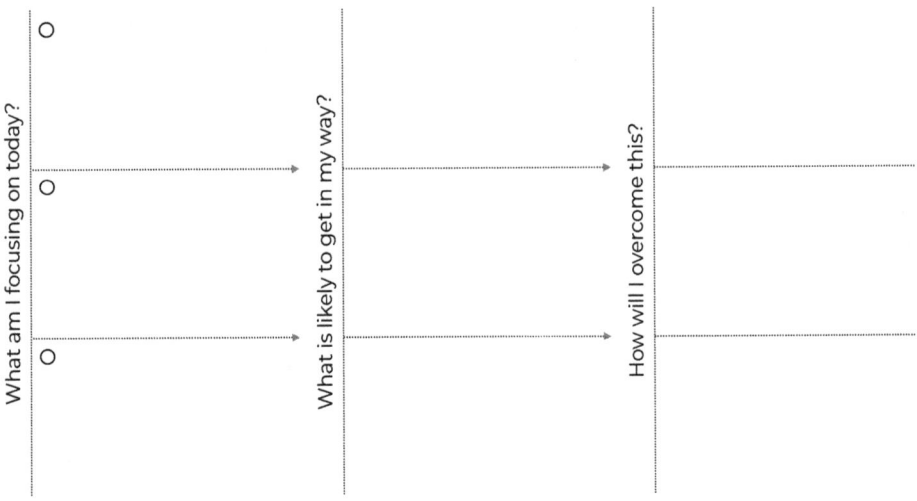

⊘ What will I say NO to today?

☾ DAILY REFLECTION

🕘 What's my favorite memory from today?

✓ Did I do what I said I would do?
What can I learn from this?

○ I reviewed my weekly tasks   TODAY'S DATE ..../........./.........

♥ I am grateful for:
Because:

☼ HOW CAN I GET A LITTLE CLOSER TO MY GOALS TODAY?

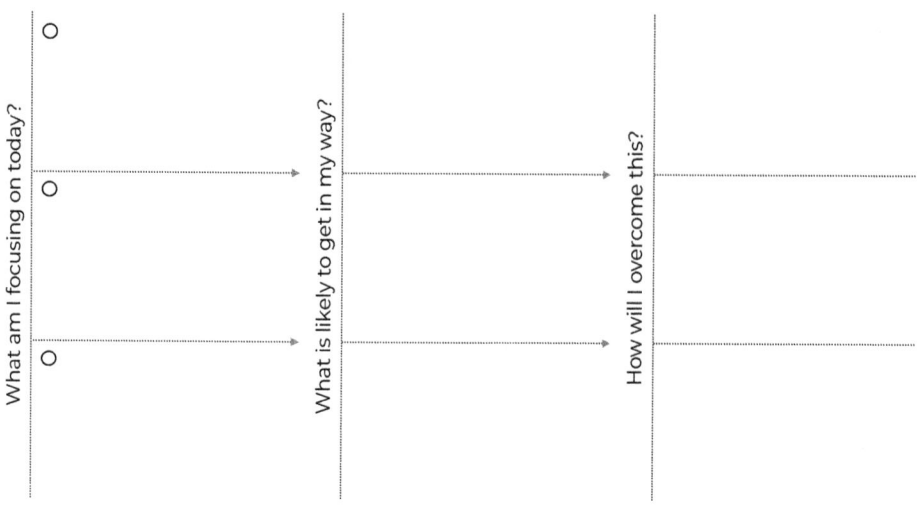

⊘ What will I say NO to today?

☾ DAILY REFLECTION

↻ What's my favorite memory from today?

✓ Did I do what I said I would do?
What can I learn from this?

○ I reviewed my weekly tasks

TODAY'S DATE ..../........../..........

♥ I am grateful for:

Because:

☀ **HOW CAN I GET A LITTLE CLOSER TO MY GOALS TODAY?**

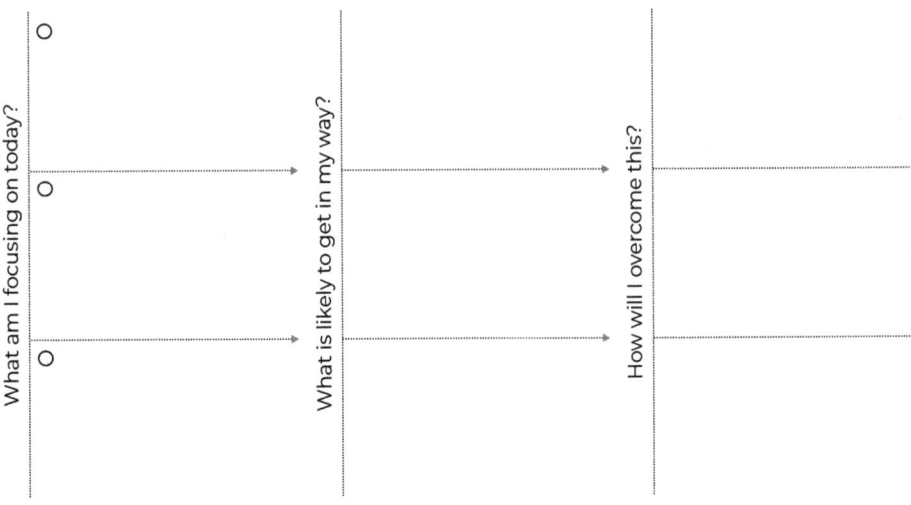

🚫 What will I say NO to today?

🌙 **DAILY REFLECTION**

🕗 What's my favorite memory from today?

✅ Did I do what I said I would do?
What can I learn from this?

◯ I reviewed my weekly tasks   TODAY'S DATE ..../.........../...........

♥ I am grateful for:
Because:

☀ HOW CAN I GET A LITTLE CLOSER TO MY GOALS TODAY?

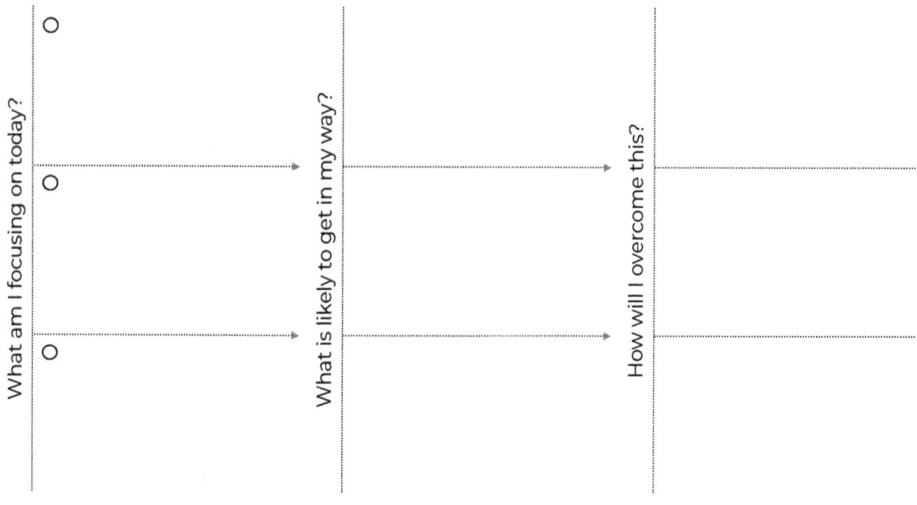

🚫 What will I say NO to today?

_____

☾ DAILY REFLECTION

🕒 What's my favorite memory from today?

✓ Did I do what I said I would do?
What can I learn from this?

○ I reviewed my weekly tasks   TODAY'S DATE _____/_____/_____

♥ I am grateful for:
Because:

☀ **HOW CAN I GET A LITTLE CLOSER TO MY GOALS TODAY?**

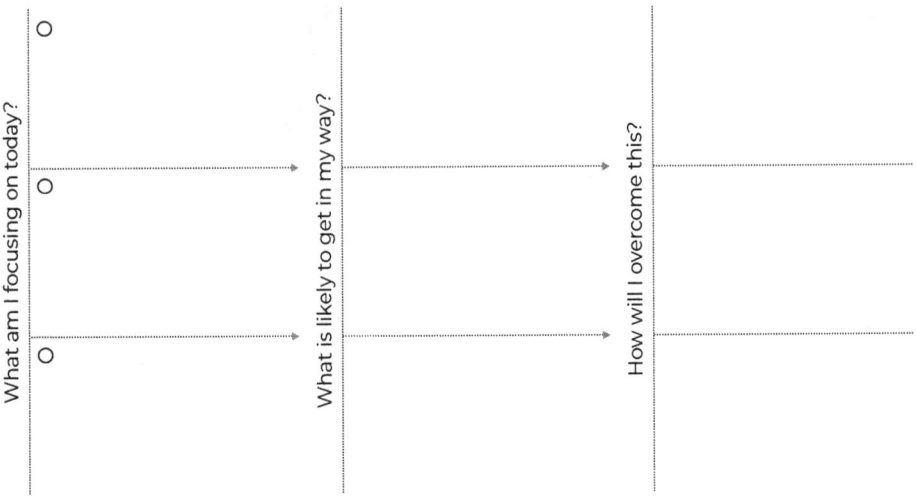

⊘ What will I say NO to today?

_____

☾ **DAILY REFLECTION**

⟲ What's my favorite memory from today?

✓ Did I do what I said I would do?
What can I learn from this?

○ I reviewed my weekly tasks   **TODAY'S DATE** ..../........../..........

♥ I am grateful for:
Because:

☀ **HOW CAN I GET A LITTLE CLOSER TO MY GOALS TODAY?**

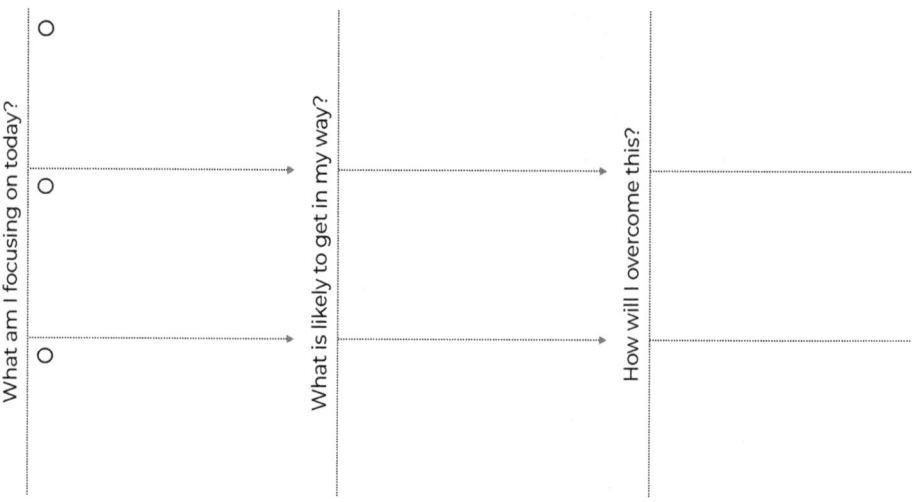

⊘ What will I say NO to today?

☾ **DAILY REFLECTION**

🕘 What's my favorite memory from today?

✓ Did I do what I said I would do?
What can I learn from this?

○ I reviewed my weekly tasks   TODAY'S DATE ..../........./.........

♥ I am grateful for:
Because:

☼ **HOW CAN I GET A LITTLE CLOSER TO MY GOALS TODAY?**

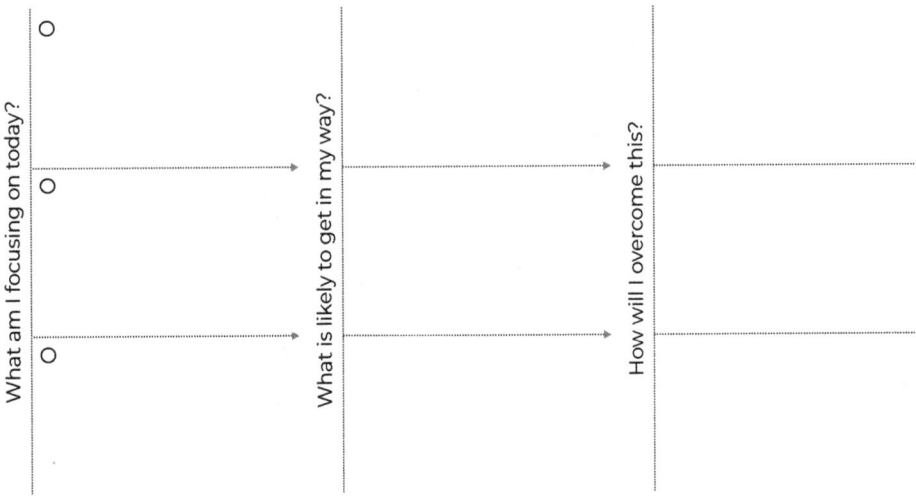

⊘ What will I say NO to today?

☾ **DAILY REFLECTION**

↺ What's my favorite memory from today?

✓ Did I do what I said I would do?
What can I learn from this?

○ I reviewed my weekly tasks   TODAY'S DATE _____/_____/_____

♥ I am grateful for:
Because:

☀ **HOW CAN I GET A LITTLE CLOSER TO MY GOALS TODAY?**

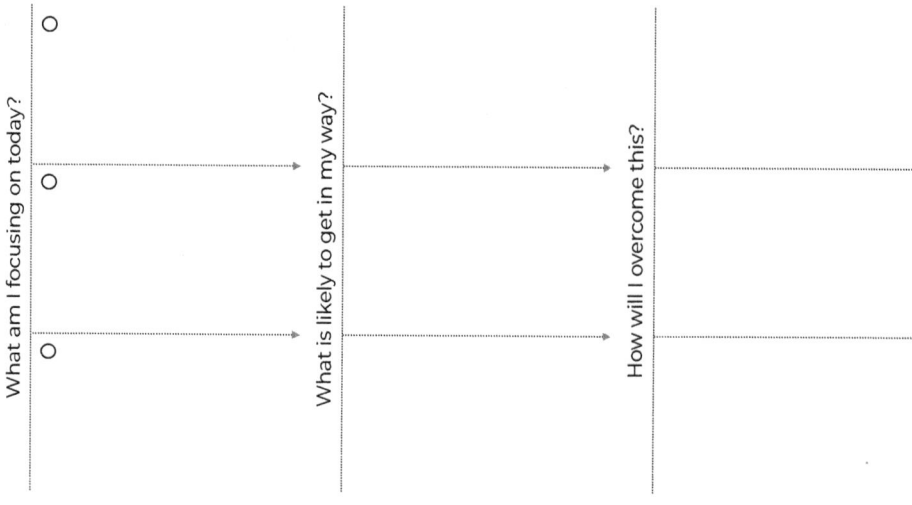

🚫 What will I say NO to today?

☾ **DAILY REFLECTION**

↺ What's my favorite memory from today?

✓ Did I do what I said I would do?
What can I learn from this?

○ I reviewed my weekly tasks   TODAY'S DATE _____ / _____ / _____

♥ I am grateful for:
Because:

☀ **HOW CAN I GET A LITTLE CLOSER TO MY GOALS TODAY?**

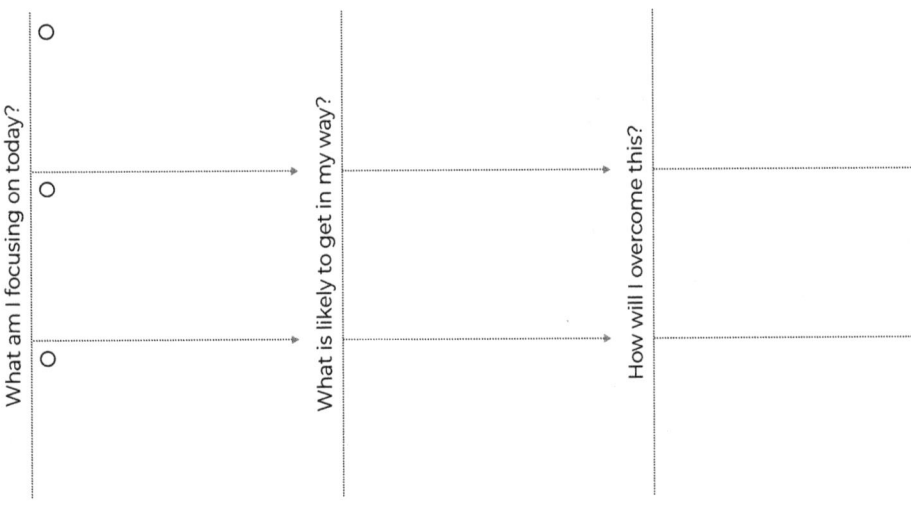

🚫 What will I say NO to today?

_____

☾ **DAILY REFLECTION**

🕘 What's my favorite memory from today?

✅ Did I do what I said I would do?
What can I learn from this?

○ I reviewed my weekly tasks

TODAY'S DATE ..../........../

♥ I am grateful for:
Because:

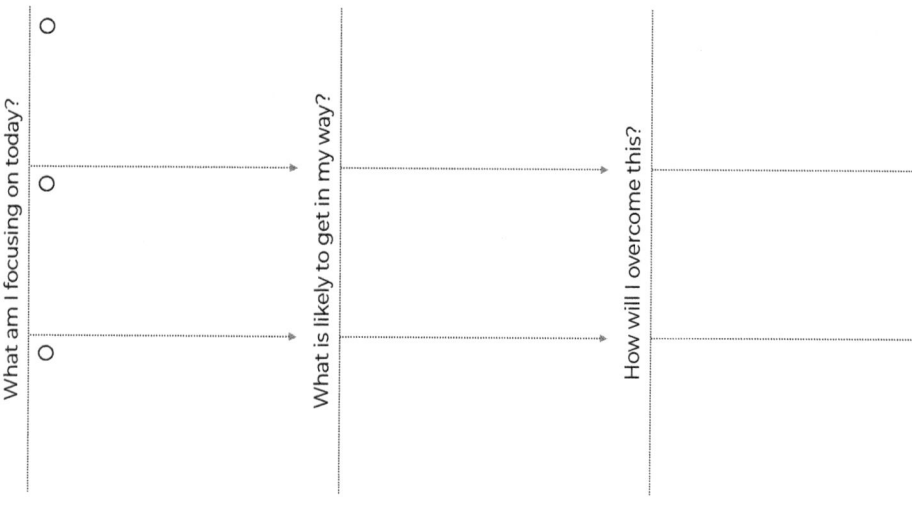

☀ HOW CAN I GET A LITTLE CLOSER TO MY GOALS TODAY?

🚫 What will I say NO to today?

🌙 DAILY REFLECTION

🕃 What's my favorite memory from today?

✅ Did I do what I said I would do?
What can I learn from this?

○ I reviewed my weekly tasks   TODAY'S DATE ..../........../..........

♥ I am grateful for:
Because:

☀ **HOW CAN I GET A LITTLE CLOSER TO MY GOALS TODAY?**

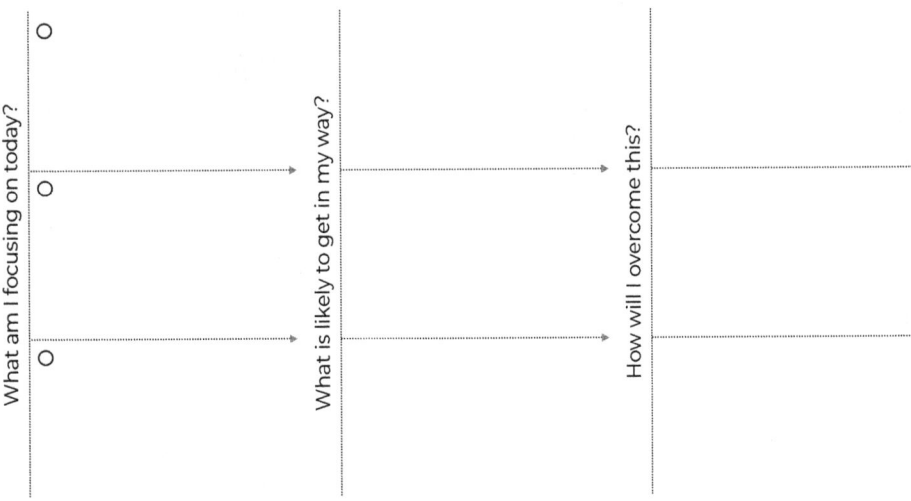

⊘ What will I say NO to today?

___

☾ **DAILY REFLECTION**

↺ What's my favorite memory from today?

✓ Did I do what I said I would do?
What can I learn from this?

○ I reviewed my weekly tasks   TODAY'S DATE ..../........./........

♥ I am grateful for:
Because:

☀ HOW CAN I GET A LITTLE CLOSER TO MY GOALS TODAY?

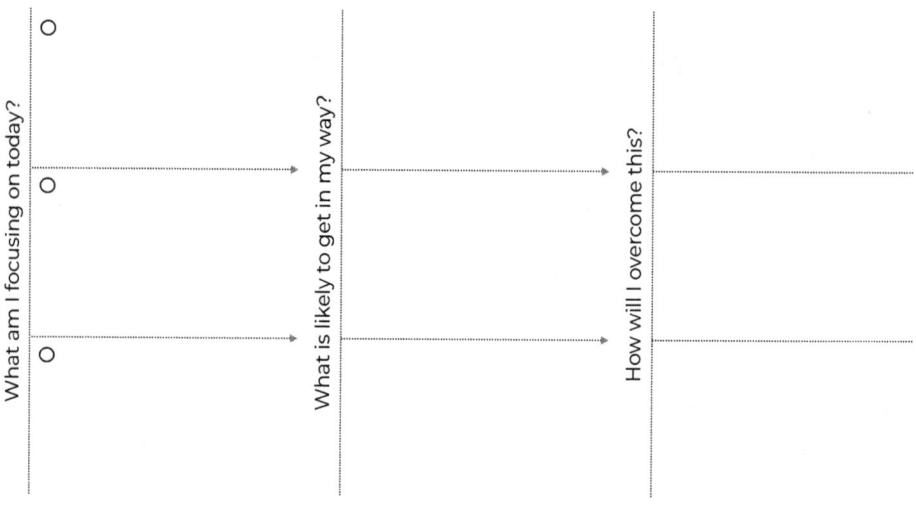

⊘ What will I say NO to today?

☾ DAILY REFLECTION

🕙 What's my favorite memory from today?

✓ Did I do what I said I would do?
What can I learn from this?

○ I reviewed my weekly tasks

TODAY'S DATE ..../........./.........

♥ I am grateful for:
Because:

☀ **HOW CAN I GET A LITTLE CLOSER TO MY GOALS TODAY?**

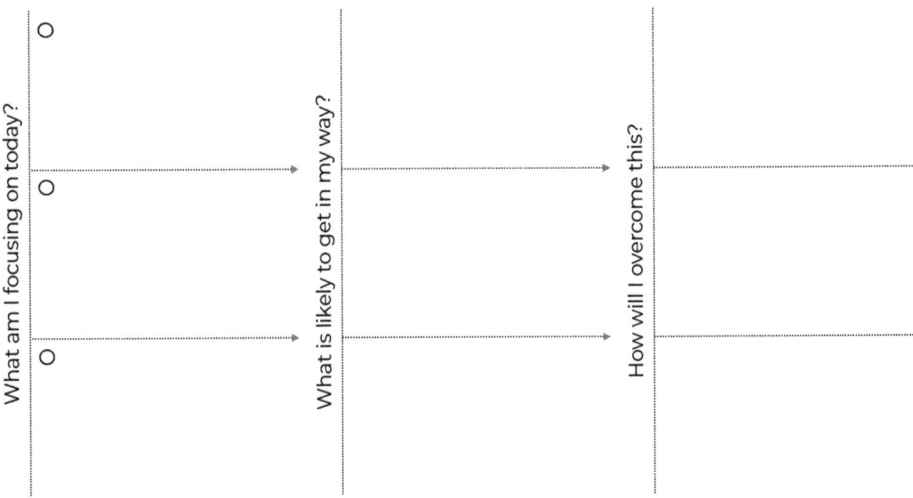

🚫 What will I say NO to today?

☾ **DAILY REFLECTION**

🕘 What's my favorite memory from today?

✔ Did I do what I said I would do?
What can I learn from this?

○ I reviewed my weekly tasks TODAY'S DATE ..../......../........

♥ I am grateful for:
Because:

☀ HOW CAN I GET A LITTLE CLOSER TO MY GOALS TODAY?

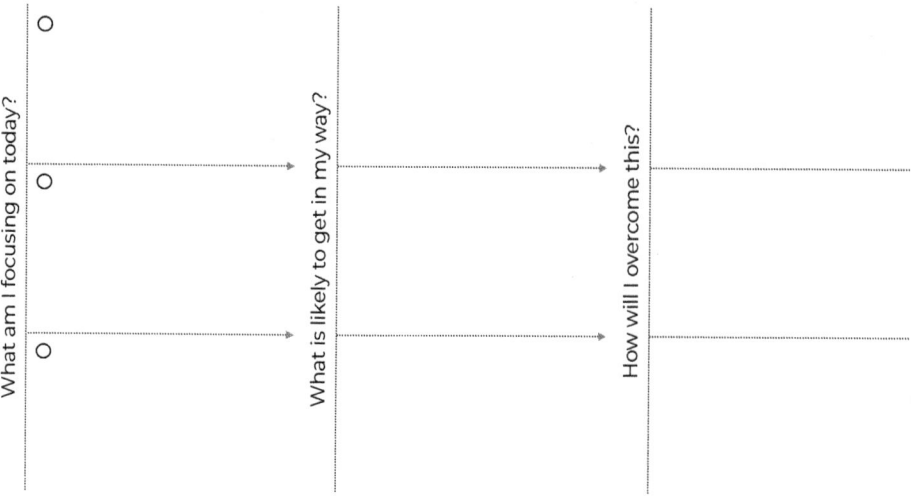

🚫 What will I say NO to today?

☾ DAILY REFLECTION

🕘 What's my favorite memory from today?

✓ Did I do what I said I would do?
What can I learn from this?

○ I reviewed my weekly tasks   TODAY'S DATE _____ / _____ / _____

♥ I am grateful for:
Because:

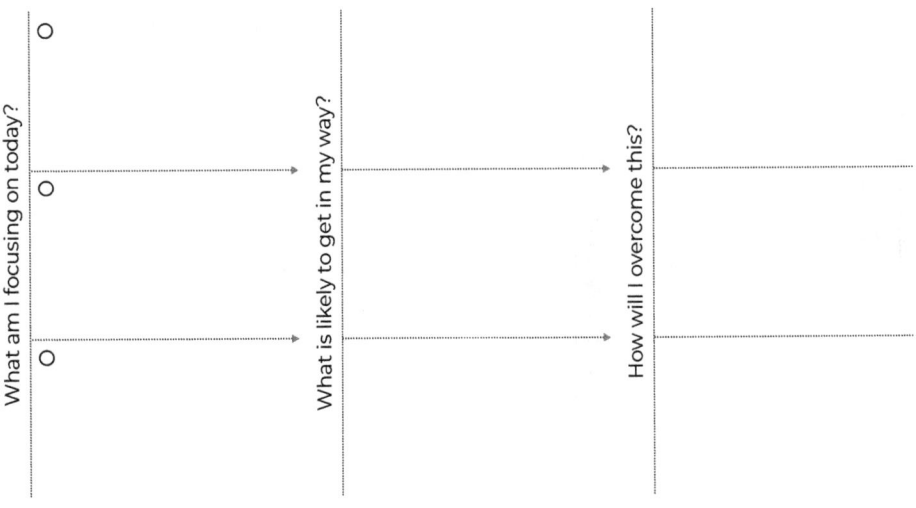

☀ **HOW CAN I GET A LITTLE CLOSER TO MY GOALS TODAY?**

🚫 What will I say NO to today?

🌙 **DAILY REFLECTION**

🕘 What's my favorite memory from today?

✓ Did I do what I said I would do?
What can I learn from this?

○ I reviewed my weekly tasks   TODAY'S DATE ..../......../

♥ I am grateful for:
Because:

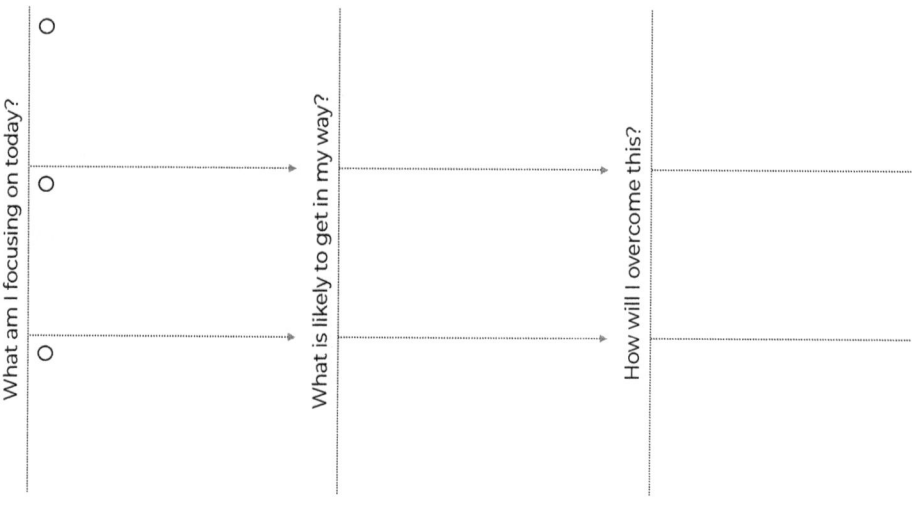

☀ HOW CAN I GET A LITTLE CLOSER TO MY GOALS TODAY?

⊘ What will I say NO to today?

☾ DAILY REFLECTION

⟲ What's my favorite memory from today?

✓ Did I do what I said I would do?
What can I learn from this?

○ I reviewed my weekly tasks   TODAY'S DATE ..../........../..........

♥ I am grateful for:
Because:

☼ **HOW CAN I GET A LITTLE CLOSER TO MY GOALS TODAY?**

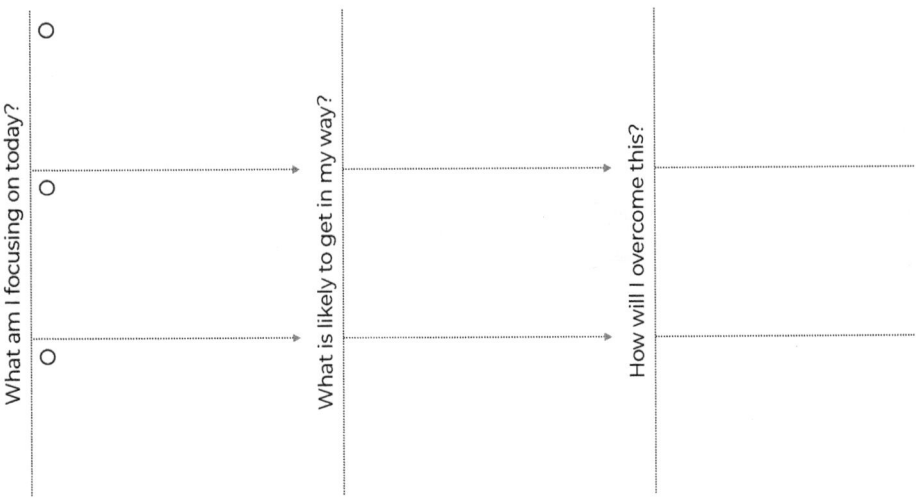

⊘ What will I say NO to today?

_____

☾ **DAILY REFLECTION**

⟲ What's my favorite memory from today?

✓ Did I do what I said I would do?
What can I learn from this?

○ I reviewed my weekly tasks   TODAY'S DATE ..../........../..........

♥ I am grateful for:
Because:

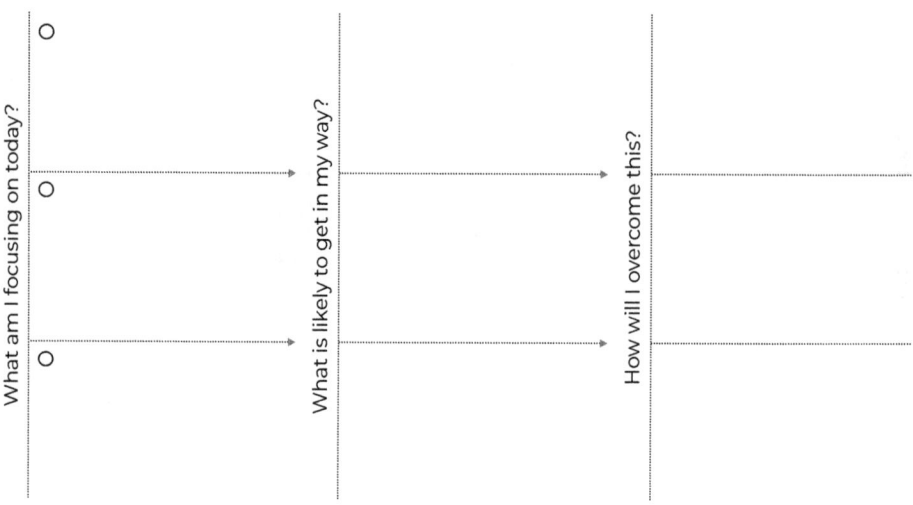

☀ **HOW CAN I GET A LITTLE CLOSER TO MY GOALS TODAY?**

⊘ What will I say NO to today?

☾ **DAILY REFLECTION**

↻ What's my favorite memory from today?

✓ Did I do what I said I would do?
What can I learn from this?

○ I reviewed my weekly tasks　　　　TODAY'S DATE ..../.........../..........

♥ I am grateful for:
Because:

☀ **HOW CAN I GET A LITTLE CLOSER TO MY GOALS TODAY?**

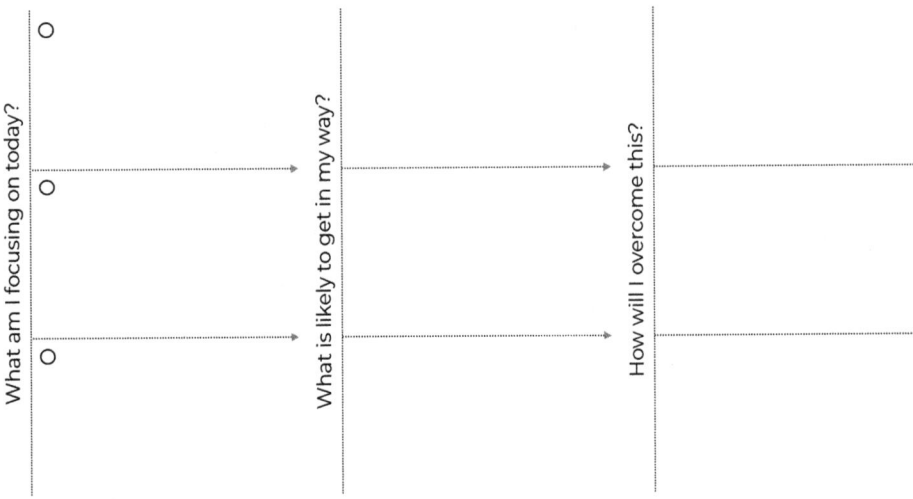

🚫 What will I say NO to today?

☾ **DAILY REFLECTION**

🕚 What's my favorite memory from today?

✅ Did I do what I said I would do?
What can I learn from this?

○ I reviewed my weekly tasks   **TODAY'S DATE** .... / .... / ....

♥ I am grateful for:

Because:

☀ HOW CAN I GET A LITTLE CLOSER TO MY GOALS TODAY?

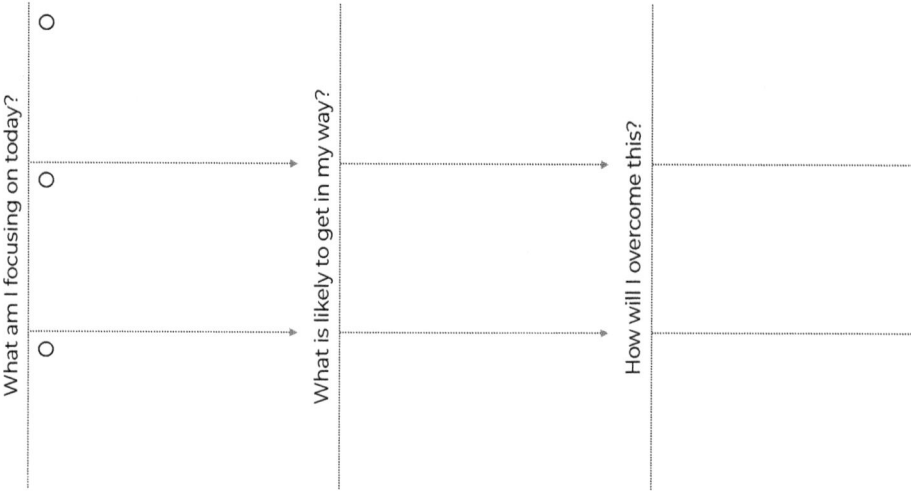

🚫 What will I say NO to today?

☾ DAILY REFLECTION

🕘 What's my favorite memory from today?

✅ Did I do what I said I would do?
What can I learn from this?

○ I reviewed my weekly tasks TODAY'S DATE _____/_____/_____

♥ I am grateful for:
Because:

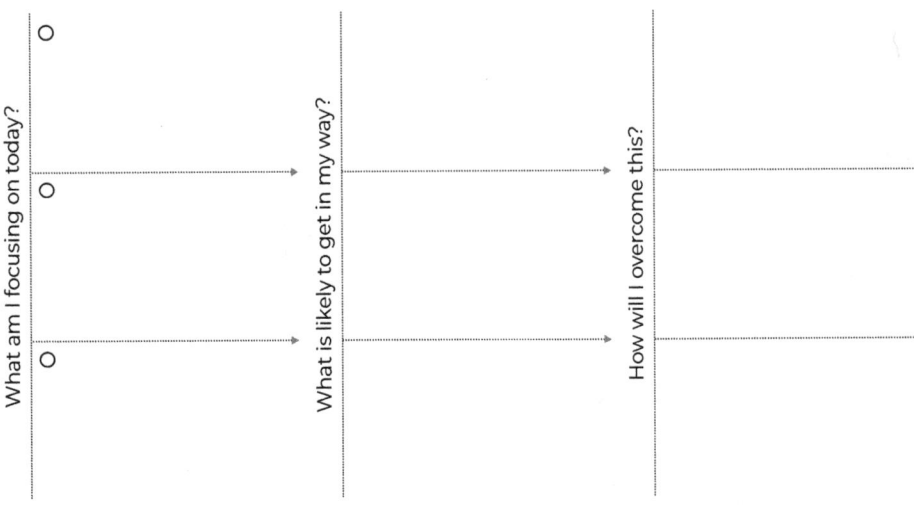

☀ **HOW CAN I GET A LITTLE CLOSER TO MY GOALS TODAY?**

🚫 What will I say NO to today?

_____

☾ **DAILY REFLECTION**

🕘 What's my favorite memory from today?

✅ Did I do what I said I would do?
What can I learn from this?

○ I reviewed my weekly tasks   TODAY'S DATE ..../........./.........

♥ I am grateful for:
Because:

☀ HOW CAN I GET A LITTLE CLOSER TO MY GOALS TODAY?

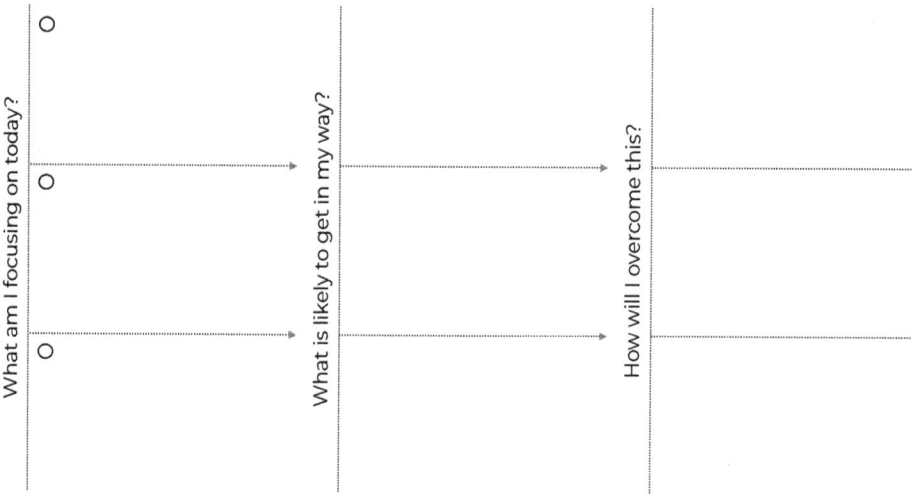

⊘ What will I say NO to today?

☾ DAILY REFLECTION

🕗 What's my favorite memory from today?

✔ Did I do what I said I would do?
What can I learn from this?

○ I reviewed my weekly tasks   TODAY'S DATE ..../........../..........

♥ I am grateful for:
Because:

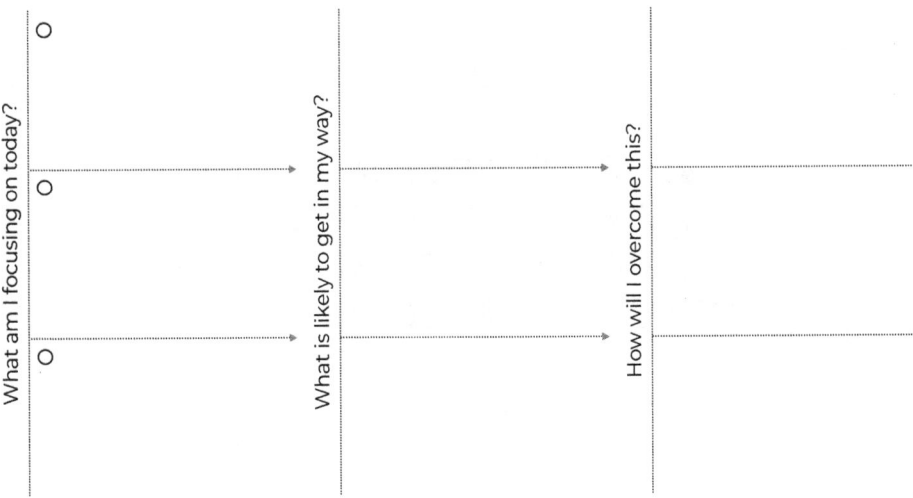

☀ **HOW CAN I GET A LITTLE CLOSER TO MY GOALS TODAY?**

⊘ What will I say NO to today?

☾ **DAILY REFLECTION**

🕑 What's my favorite memory from today?

✓ Did I do what I said I would do?
What can I learn from this?

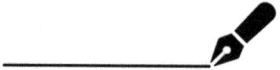

WHAT LIES BEHIND YOU AND WHAT LIES IN FRONT OF YOU, PALES IN COMPARISON TO WHAT LIES INSIDE YOU.

—Ralph Waldo Emerson

REFLECT ON YOUR 90-DAY GOALS

DOING GREAT WORK IS A powerful, life-changing practice. You stuck with it all the way to the end! I'm impressed, and you should be, too.

Now it's time to look back, reflect, and learn.

♥ Savor the Good

The best part of using this journal just might very well be the record you now have of your favorite memories and gratitudes. Spend time savoring them as you reflect upon the last 90 days.

🔭 Celebrate Your Progress

You're moving in the right direction, and you are learning along the way. It's really easy to minimize your wins and focus on where you still have room to grow. Don't do that! Focus most of your energy on the progress you are making, as that's what creates momentum and gives you that warm feeling of satisfaction.

☺ Be Excited About Where You're Headed

No matter how much you improve, there will always be room to grow. This isn't a bad thing! How boring would life be if you had everything figured out? Well, no worries there! It's not possible. The key, here, is to enjoy the ride.

🚶 Keep Going

This is just the beginning! The real magic happens when aligning your time to your Great Work becomes a way of life. After you reflect on where you've been, grab your next Great Work Journal, and plan for the next 90-days!

Get your next Great Work Journal and the Great Work Resource Pack at amandacrowell.com/Great-Work-Journal

🕒 **My favorite memories from the past 90 days are:**

1	2	3
3	4	5

How did I do against my goals? Did I do them? What can I learn from this?

◎ **Stretch Goal:**
Learning:

◎ **Support Goal:**
Learning:

◎ **Sanity Goal:**
Learning:

💡 **What did I learn about myself as I pursued these goals?**

🎯 90-DAY REFLECTION: WEB OF LIFE

Using the same circles you used during your 90-day planning, re-assess your Web of Life. **Remember:**

1. **Mark how satisfied you are in this area of your life** by placing a dot on the line between the word "low" and the circle. The closer to the word "low," the less satisfied you are. Connect the dots with a line to see your web of satisfaction.
2. **Rank order them from 1-12 according to their priority to you.** On the line next to each circle, give each area a rank order. Force yourself to choose between items that feel identical in their priority to you.

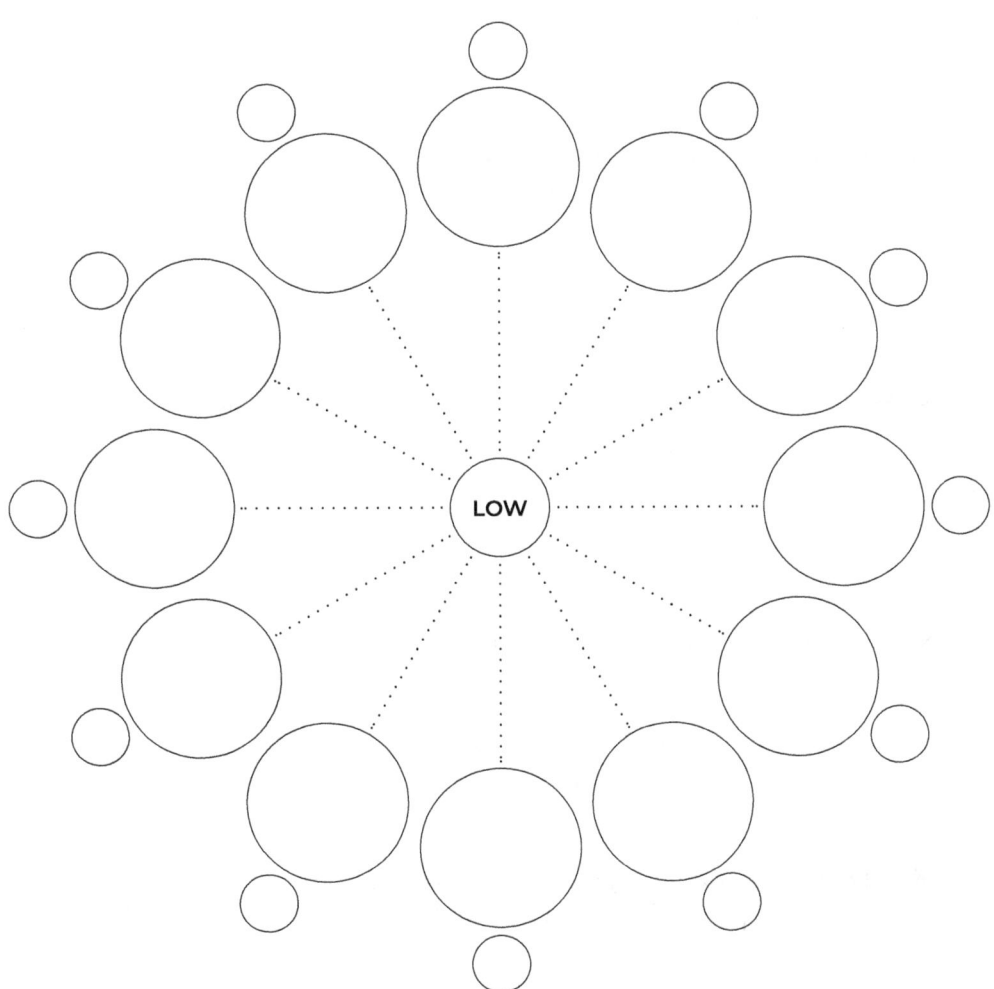

Now, look at your updated Web of Life and notice what you notice.

📈 Did I have the impact I was hoping for?

📌 What still needs some attention?

☺ When I was at my best in the past 90 days, what words described me?

⏵ What were my biggest breakthroughs from the past 90 days?

♥ For what am I most grateful from the past 90 days?

🔖 As I begin the next 90 days, what am I keeping in mind?

 NOTES

 **NOTES**

 **NOTES**

NOTES

NOTES

NOTES

NOTES

www.ingramcontent.com/pod-product-compliance
Lightning Source LLC
Chambersburg PA
CBHW051851160426
43209CB00006B/1255